# BREW A BATCH

## A BEGINNER'S GUIDE TO HOME-BREWED BEER

# BREW A BATCH

## A BEGINNER'S GUIDE TO HOME-BREWED BEER

*Christopher Sidwa*

**MURDOCH BOOKS**

SYDNEY · LONDON

# CONTENTS

# Howdy!

Welcome to home brewing. Whether you've brewed before or are just starting out, I'm happy to be part of your discovery of flavour and creativity.

I discovered home brewing by accident. Back in 1998, as a university student in Connecticut, the cheap, flavourless mass-produced beers I was drinking frustrated me. A resurgence in craft beer had seen a rise in small independent American breweries, so I set off to look for something different in my local bottle shop. I walked past the 'premium' imports like Guinness (too thick and dark: won't that fill me up?*) and local offerings like Samuel Adams (too fancy), before stumbling upon cider. It seemed to be good value, was an alternative to what I was drinking, and I figured it would go down a treat with my late-night calzone order.

After a few weekends slurping cider, I began to wonder what it would take to turn the apples being sold at roadside stalls into my new boozy beverage of choice. A quick trip to my university library (yes, this was before broadband internet), revealed cider was the drink favoured by early European settlers in my area of Connecticut, but there was no book in the uni library explaining how to make alcoholic cider, so I checked out the bookstore in my local mall. There, in amongst the cookbooks and 'how to' books, was a home-brewing book, and in it was a chapter on cider. So I bought the book and took it home.

Had I been patient enough to glance over more than just its table of contents, I would have saved myself a few bucks — and never ventured down one of the most exciting paths of my life. The second paragraph of the cider chapter told me a crucial piece of information, which to this day has kept me from ever making cider: a good cider can take months to mature. *Months?!* I was a university student. My life at the time was broken down into three-month semesters. I couldn't wait an entire semester for my grog to be ready — so I stopped reading and put the book on the shelf.

* No, it wouldn't! The appearance and mouthfeel of Guinness are deceiving. From a technical perspective it's very dry, low in alcohol and therefore relatively low in calories. Rookie mistake on my part.

As I'd later discover, the book, *Homebrewing for Dummies* by Marty Nachel, contained some of the most practical advice a new brewer could ever want. In fact, if there hadn't been so many innovations in brewing in the two decades or so since that book's publication, I wouldn't even be writing this one. But with creative boundaries being pushed, technology advancing the way it has, and the ever-rising interest in authentic, flavoursome well-crafted beers, it's time for another story.

That book travelled with me after finishing uni, along with an interest in learning how to create something from scratch.

Armed with an economics degree, I fumbled around with a few odd jobs, selling Christmas trees, delivering flowers, valet-parking cars — all the while considering what it was I really wanted to do. Thankfully, I was living in a town with a brew pub. On Thursday nights they sold bottles of tasteless macro lager for $1, to pull people in and expose them to their line-up of full-flavoured, house-made beers. Their strategy worked — first on me, then on my friends.

Sitting amongst wood-cladded fermenters, listening to the gentle bubbling of fermenting beer, I had my beer epiphany over a pint of their malt-driven, English-style brown ale. The brewer, who was from my neighbourhood, was making a living and raising his family while contributing to our town and giving people something to get excited about. I thought that was pretty cool. But following something as interesting as a career in beer was too big of a gamble for me at the time, so the idea of brewing my own beers was relegated to a hobby.

Conveniently, the owners of the pub ran a small home-brew shop in a room upstairs with all the essentials. I dusted off my old home-brew book, got my first real job with a bank in New York City and spent my first pay cheque on home-brewing equipment.

And so my own home-brew journey began. I'd lay down a new batch of beer about once a month, and while I had a few disasters, there weren't too many — mainly because I had a good brewing book and I followed it to a T. Boring but true!

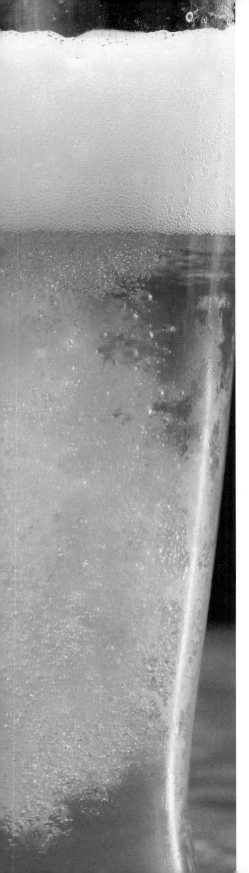

After a decade of steadily fine-tuning my process, in late 2013 I invested my life savings, alongside my business partner, to launch Batch Brewing Co in the Sydney suburb of Marrickville.

A truckload of other things had also happened in those ten years, including a job transfer to Sydney, Australia. But just two months after moving my partner and our lives across the world, my team in Sydney was made redundant, and I was left running an investment portfolio in Australia by myself. It was a slow, lonely and soulless job, but I enjoyed the challenge. On the plus side, I had plenty of time to brew beer and study the brewing process, digesting every book I could get my hands on.

Home brewing and commercial brewing are two very different animals, and while I was confident in my ability to make small batches in my kitchen, I was not naive enough to believe I could turn a hobby into a viable business. The commercial brewing industry is incredibly competitive and multifaceted, so in my mind brewing would remain a daydream and something to revisit when the banking industry finally had enough of me.

But as fate would have it, I met Andrew Fineran, another American in Sydney, who worked for a major Australian brewer. We found ourselves to have a very similar vision of a brewery that would be unique to Sydney, as well as having complementary skills: he matched my operational, financial and brewing knowledge with an understanding of the concept of brand — and marketing that brand — I'd never even considered.

We brewed batch after batch in his backyard, and despite regular interruptions from his curious toddler, who survived explorations of our boiling kettle with her fingers intact (a future brewer perhaps!), we carved out an idea, and knocked over barriers fine-tuning our flavours, values, personality and finances. What emerged was a business plan, beer prototypes, a truly collaborative partnership — and a whole new life and brewing journey for us and our families.

We upgraded from a 45 litre (12 gallon) home-brew kit to a 1200 litre (317 gallon) system, and while it was still a big gamble, our mission was clear: to contribute to, and collaborate with, our local community, while enriching lives by making great-tasting beer. Whether I'm brewing for friends, family or the wider community, it's always been paramount that the processes and ingredients I use respect my suppliers, my neighbours, my drinkers and the beer community.

So why might *you* brew? Every home brewer's story is unique, but I've found there are a few common themes.

The first is the desire to create something that's not commercially available. The offerings at your local beer outlet may be broad, or limited — but even at the best-stocked shops I'm certain there's a wide range of beer variations they don't offer.

The second is the satisfaction you get from sharing what you've created with others. In our busy lives we focus on making our bosses happy and simply providing for our families. But when we allow ourselves the time to create, quite often we find a new sense of happiness and satisfaction that we want to share.

Also, home brewing enables endless creativity, with limited risk. If you want to make a beer that sounds great to you but terrible to your mates, go for it! You're only making 19 litres (5 gallons), so you can afford to take a gamble. Throw in your favourite childhood candy and surprise your friends. And hey, maybe they were right and it *does* taste awful. Who cares? Forget what other people want, what do *you* want? Create without risk. And without boundaries.

No two drinking experiences are ever exactly the same. And as you go through your own brewing journey, you will find yourself collecting these experiences, banking them in your flavour memory, and drawing on them for inspiration as you set out to craft your perfect beer.

So let's get started.

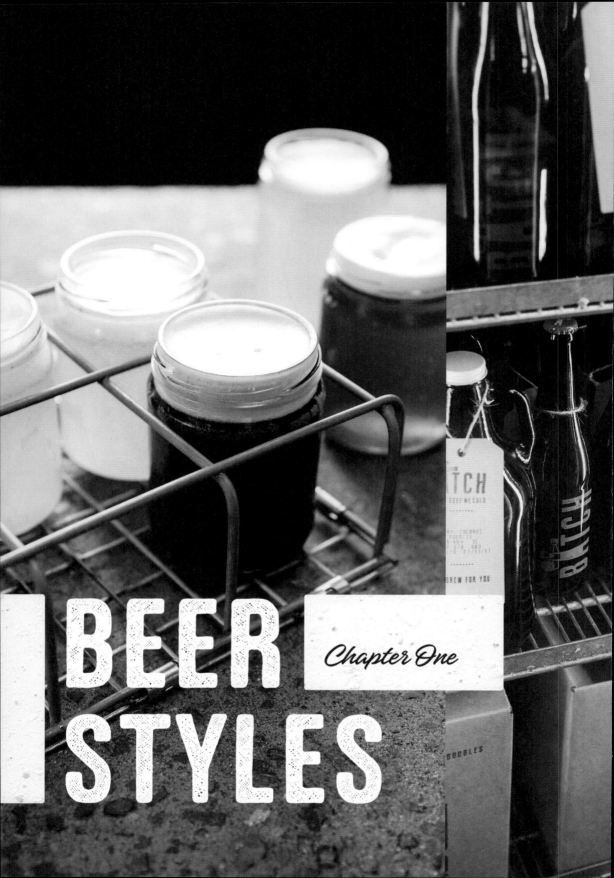

# BEER STYLES

*Chapter One*

We can't talk about brewing beer without first talking about beer styles. We need to have an idea of *what* we're trying to make, before we set off making it.

Beer is categorised based on its colour, flavour, intensity and visual appearance, and the ingredients used to make it. Descriptors like pale or dark, sweet or dry, hoppy, bitter and fruity are all great for communicating what you want your beer to taste like — but not what style you want it to be.

Thankfully, generations of brewers before us have identified the many different beers into clearly defined categories, so we can have a much simpler conversation about what beer we want to make.

Beer can be broken down into two main styles: ale and lager. What separates the two is the type of yeast used to ferment the beer, and how long the yeast needs to do its thing.

## Ales

Ales are made using yeast strains that are most productive at a relatively warm temperature — around 19°C (66°F). Because these yeast strains are allowed to work at warmer temperatures, they complete their ferment process faster, leaving behind more pronounced flavour.

Some styles of ale are ready to be consumed in as little as 10 days, or as many as 16 days.

Let's take a closer look at the different styles of ale.

### PALE ALES

The traditional Pale Ale is pale in colour, with a slight herbal hop aroma, and is fermented using ale yeast. Its big brother is India Pale Ale, which was born in the 1800s when soldiers of the British Empire stationed in India were thirsty for beer that suited the hot climate and yet tasted of home. This new beer, brewed in England to be consumed in India, depended on the inherent anti-microbial properties of hops to keep the beer-spoiling bacteria at bay on its six-month journey across the Equator and around the Horn of Africa. The result was a very hoppy

| Examples of Ales | Examples of Lagers |
| --- | --- |
| * Pale ale<br>* Amber ale<br>* Brown ale<br>* Porter<br>* Stout<br>* Weizen or wheat ale | * Helles, or pale<br>* Pilsner<br>* Vienna, or amber<br>* Bock<br>* Schwartzbier, or dark |

pale ale that was brewed with extra alcohol, another mitigant against bacterial contamination.

In the quest to drive creativity and capture drinkers' attention, marketers have come up with some wild names of late: XPA (Extra Pale Ale), Double IPA, Triple IPA, New England IPA. Under the new guard of headline-grabbing brewers, we've expanded this genre from Pale Ale and India Pale Ale to something that is impossible to untangle. Whether your low-alcohol, hoppy beer is a session IPA or an XPA, it's still pale and uses lots of hops. And while I personally have brewed, marketed and sold beer with the monikers listed above, I think most don't need to exist.

The chart opposite gives an approximate breakdown of each.

A 'dry hop' is a quantity of hops added to the beer while it's in a fermentation vessel, to impart extra aroma and flavour into the beer.

Original gravity (OG) is the amount of sugar in the wort before yeast is added. Final gravity (FG) is the amount of sugar remaining after fermentation is complete. By comparing these values, a brewer can calculate the amount of alcohol created by the yeast.

## AMBER ALE

On the spectrum of beer colours, the next shade darker than Pale Ale is Amber Ale. These beers get their colour through the addition of malts that have been roasted to varying degrees, deepening their colour and intensifying their flavours. As we add more of these malts, we move from a pale colour to golden, then amber.

**Pale Ale probably originated in England in the early 1700s. Before that time darker beers, such as porters and stouts, were more common, due to the wood (and then coal) used to heat the malting kilns, which darkened the grains and added colour to the malt and subsequent beer. However, as beer-making technology advanced, it became easier to create a paler malt, and pale ales gradually became more popular than the darker ales.**

| | English Pale Ale | American Pale Ale | Session IPA | XPA | IPA | Double IPA | New England IPA |
|---|---|---|---|---|---|---|---|
| **Bittering** | Moderate | Moderate | Subdued | Subdued | For balance | For balance | Minimal |
| **Aroma** | Moderate | Moderate | Potent | Potent | Strong | Very strong | Strong |
| **Dry hop** | Present | Moderate | Heavy | Heavy | Strong | Twice, in sizable quantities | Twice, large, during primary ferment |
| **OG (original gravity)** | 1.040 | 1.050 | 1.045 | 1.045 | 1.060 | 1.080 | 1.070 |
| **FG (final gravity)** | 1.012 | 1.010 | 1.010 | 1.010 | 1.012 | 1.016 | 1.016 |

As in the world of Pale Ale, there is ambiguity around what qualifies as Amber Ale. Once upon a time, beer labelled Amber Ale implied it was 'malt forward' — meaning the first flavour experience would be malt, followed by a minimal hop presence. That's no longer the case. Now, we have traditional, low-bitterness English-style amber-coloured beers, and we have big imperial ambers with 8% alcohol and a high bitterness rating.

My suggestion is to pay little attention to what style guidelines require of your amber ale and focus on what flavour you want to create.

Want a hoppy amber ale? Research your hops and find one to complement the rich flavour added by the roasted malt, or the residual sweetness from a dark crystal malt. Once you decide what your beer will be, learn to communicate those flavours, so your drinkers understand what the beer is intending to do. Does it show nuance and balance of malt and hop? Or is it sticky sweet, to carry the huge charge of hops you added at the end of the boil? Both can be amber ales — the trick is to give your drinker more info so they understand what they're getting and can judge your beer based on that, and not on a generic term like 'amber ale'.

## BROWN ALE

Sometimes called 'the pinot noir of beer', Brown Ale is an incredibly versatile style that drinks well on its own, and pairs with a broad range of foods. Like Amber Ales, Brown Ales can be either 'hop forward' or 'malt forward'. Their defining flavour comes from the use of chocolate malt — a type of malt roasted to a point where chocolate flavours are created.

Good Brown Ale should also create a perception of malty sweetness, without a high level of residual sugar. Traditionally, the style used hops sparingly to create a balance of sweet and bitter, but leaned towards malty and sweet. Excellent examples of this style exist in the relatively low 4% alcohol range, but fuller, bigger versions can drink very nicely at 6%.

The malty base of Brown Ale can also be an excellent base to experiment with adding various spices, teas and fruits to your brew.

## PORTER AND STOUT

The use of brown malt traditionally defined these styles, but economics, taxation and technology advancements in the early 1800s saw a combination of pale malt and heavily roasted black malt being used instead. Some traditionalists still believe in the addition of brown malt, but a good Porter or Stout doesn't require it.

The line between a Porter and a Stout is vague. A 'Stout Porter' was once a strong porter — a beer brewed with the same ingredients, but to a richer flavour and higher alcohol level than regular porter. Eventually the term Porter was dropped from the name, and Stout emerged as a stand-alone style. Since then, wars, tax policy and consumer tastes have moved the strength of stouts down to where porter traditionally sat. Today, you could be forgiven for calling your black beer a Porter or a Stout. But once again, don't get hung up on names. Understanding your ingredients and what each fermentable offers in terms of colour, texture and flavour will get you closer to making great-tasting beer than memorising style guidelines for what makes a porter or a stout.

**WHEAT ALE**

This style was once defined by the use of malted wheat, coupled with a yeast strain that produced flavours of banana and clove. The traditional Hefeweizen (*hefe* means 'yeast' and *weizen* means 'wheat' in German) is still wildly popular, but the Wheat Ale category has grown to include wheat-based beers fermented with yeast strains that express different flavours.

There are the fairly yeast-forward versions like the traditional Belgian Witbier, and more modern hop-forward versions being produced by innovative American craft brewers. So what determines a wheat beer these days is simply that the brewer uses about half wheat as the grain component in their brew — the yeast, hops and other flavours are totally up to the brewer.

# Lagers

A word of caution before we spend too much time on lagers: I want everyone who reads this book to be successful in their brewing journey. Attempting to brew lager beers before developing and refining your process for making ale is like learning to ride a bike in traffic up a hill. Why set out to do it the hard way? Definitely start by nailing your ales first, then venture into lagers later.

The word 'lager' means 'to store' in its native German. The yeast strain selected is happiest working in relatively cool temperatures — around 10ºC (50ºF). Being a living organism, yeast, like us, moves a bit more slowly when it's cold. This slower ferment leads to a less pronounced flavour profile than you'll experience in an ale. Lager beer must be stored for enough time, and at a cool enough temperature, for this particular yeast to complete its work. In many cases this means 5–6 weeks, but it can be as many as 12 weeks or more.

So, the features that distinguish lagers from ales are the time used to make them, the temperature at which they are fermented, and the yeast strains used (which have been selected because they work at these lower temperatures).

Helles,
or pale

Vienna,
or amber

Bock

Schwartzbier,
or dark

**The process of storing beer cold and allowing it to mature traces back to Germany, where brewers would have naturally 'captured' a yeast that thrived in cold temperatures — and then, over time, cultivated that yeast, which became known as 'lager yeast'.**

By volume, the vast majority of beer produced in the world is lager, and it's fair to say that most of that volume falls into the pale lager category. Despite a huge number of taps being dedicated to a seemingly broad range of brands, the beer styles poured from those taps fall into a very narrow range of pale lagers. Within this narrow sliver, the lagers distinguish themselves pretty much only on their marketing and calorie content, because there is in fact very little that distinguishes them from one another as beers.

The world of lager spans from pale to black. Lagers can be just as versatile in their flavours and ingredients as ales. They can be 'malt forward', or have a firm hop presence, and can use smoked malt, wheat, rye and oats.

Lagers are made by leaving the beer for a long period of time at cold temperatures. During this process, the yeast continues to evolve and mellow the flavour of the beer. Haze-forming particles drop out of suspension, giving the beer a brightness and clarity not found in ales.

To make lager at home you need a dedicated refrigeration space, which is expensive and takes a bit of room. Having a second fridge in your kitchen may work if you live alone or with thirsty housemates, but it takes a special partner to be that supportive of your hobby. You are also committing your fermentation space to one beer for many weeks, or even months. So rather than getting a lot of repetitions at brewing, and getting better at your craft, you're waiting for your beer to finish. These constraints make lagers tough to tackle at first.

But when you're ready to give them a try, they can be incredibly rewarding, and are worth the extra effort. With quick and warm ale fermentation, certain flavours get created by the yeast that become the signature of ale. During the long, slow maturation period of lager, the yeast reabsorbs or converts many of the flavour compounds it initially excreted, leaving a flavour that can be described as clean or mellow. Also, during the aging and conditioning period, hop flavour subsides.

Some innovative brewers have attempted hoppy lagers with great success, but traditionally lagers have been malt-focused beers. They offer a crisp and refreshing alternative to the aggressively hopped ales. I'm not saying those hop-forward beers are inferior — I'm just saying that variety is great, and a well-executed lager can be a rewarding drop.

## Beer and taxes

You can't talk about beer styles without talking about government and taxes.

Throughout time, beer styles have been dictated by what brewers could produce in a commercially viable way. In 1516 the Bavarian government imposed rules around what ingredients could be used to make beer — only hops, malted barley, water and yeast — and those restrictions have influenced an entire beer culture for over 500 years. The rules were set to protect Bavarian beers from imported products, and to placate conservatives who didn't like some products made with hop alternatives being used in pagan rituals. The impact: a loss of creativity and flavour innovation.

Sometimes tax policy is abused as an easy way for governments to raise revenue; people want their beer, and will pay a little more if they must. And sometimes tax policy is designed to attempt to affect your behaviour by limiting your alcohol intake. In this case, the price of beer increases as its alcohol content rises, making big, boozy beers very expensive and relegating them to special occasions. Since this restricts the size of the market for these expensive beers, they aren't made commercially too often. But they can be very tasty and are the perfect thing to brew at home.

When you're considering what style of beer to brew, keep in mind that what the textbooks say a style should be is often the result of some tax officer making a taxation rule that commercial brewers base their beers around. So don't read the style guides too literally — as a home brewer, you can take whatever creative liberties you want, and base your beers around flavour and the ingredients you have access to.

# THE
# PROCESS

*Chapter Two*

# From humble beginnings...

The earliest beers were probably made by accident.

A carbohydrate-rich seed would have blown or fallen into a vessel that captured water, the moisture tricking the seed into thinking it was time to grow — thus kicking off the natural germination process, which involves converting starch into simpler sugars. Naturally existing yeast and bacteria would have found their way into the watery mixture, feeding on the fermentable sugars, in the process converting those sugars into alcohol and carbon dioxide. Then some brave, or hungry, soul would have tasted the fizzy brew, gotten a buzz and wanted more!

The beer's flavour would have been a result of compounds imparted by the yeast, sour acids left behind by the bacteria, and sugar that the yeast hadn't consumed yet. Further batches would have been made by adding more fermentable materials to what was left behind in the vessel from the last batch, or by transferring the yeast and bacteria from batch to batch on a porous wooden stick.

Over thousands of years, processes were fine-tuned, and supply chains set up to support the production of better beer. Some archaeologists say civilisation itself was created by the need to domesticate cereal plants to support the growing demand for beer!

These refinements meant resources could be used more efficiently to create greater volumes of better-tasting beer. Thankfully, we modern brewers get to stand on the shoulders of all those who have come before us. We don't have to fumble through experiments to learn how to make good beer — this book should start you on that journey. Instead we have the privilege of continuing to push and evolve our local beer cultures by challenging existing thinking and trialling new ways of doing things.

## ...to big beer

It's important to keep in mind that beer is fairly simple to make. Nature does the heavy lifting; we just need to make sure the right things happen in the right order. The yeast will handle the rest.

But when you visit a modern industrial brewery, things will look a lot more complicated. That's because they're set up to reduce bacterial contamination, streamline processing and minimise excessive batch-to-batch variability. As the batch sizes increase over time, the cost of failure also increases — and once the cost of failure exceeds the cost of an extra device or technology to control a particular process, that new equipment will be employed. Over time, these technological innovations have taken modern breweries to a place that bears no resemblance to what the minimal requirements are to make beer.

So, what are those minimal requirements?

Nature does the heavy lifting; we just need to make sure the right things happen in the right order.

# From inspiration to fermentation: how beer is made

The process can be broken down into eight steps.

## 1. DEVISING A RECIPE

As with most things that are made or created, beer begins as an idea in someone's head. With beer, turning that idea into something tangible means writing a recipe. The various ingredients are pulled together based on the flavour and texture of the beer you want to make, and your knowledge, from experience and trial and error, of the kind of ingredients that will get you there.

The recipe is then refined and recorded — because brewing is nothing without good record keeping.

## 2. MILLING THE GRAIN

With recipe in hand, brewers take their malt — the primary source of the beer's fermentable sugars — to their mill to crack the kernels, exposing the starch inside. (Malt is simply the term for a cereal grain that has been allowed to germinate briefly, before being dried using varying degrees of heat.)

When milling, it's important to ensure the grains are sufficiently cracked — but not pulverised into flour. Over-crushing will damage the grain husk (the outer shell of some cereal grains), enabling unwanted 'off' flavours to leach out of the malt, into the beer. Over-crushed grain husks will also be difficult to separate out from the liquid later on.

## 3. MASHING: HOW ABOUT SOME PORRIDGE?

The cracked malt is transferred to a mash tun, where it's mixed with water at a specific temperature — warmer if the brewer wants a fuller, sweeter beer, and colder if the brewer wants a thinner, drier beer.

A mash tun is a simple insulated vessel designed to hold the mash (the mix of grains and water) and maintain its temperature. Some more sophisticated mash tuns have a heat source that enables them to control and hold a constant temperature.

It's in the mash tun that the starches in the malt are converted into sugars, in a process known as saccharification. This occurs naturally due to the existence of enzymes in the malt, which are released from the grains when mixed with water. Different types of malt contain different quantities of these enzymes, which can dramatically affect the amount of time needed to achieve the desired level of conversion from starch into 'complex sugars', and then further still into more fermentable 'simple sugars'. (Modern plant breeding has led to malts that can convert in as little as 15 minutes, although 60 minutes is a more traditional length of time.)

Complex sugars are those that yeast can't ferment, which will then carry all the way through to your drinker's glass, leaving a sweet taste in your beer.

Using low-enzyme malt, or mashing at a warmer temperature, will leave more complex sugar molecules and a sweeter beer. Using high-enzyme malt at a cool temperature will lead to happy and active enzymes that are able to more readily chop those starches and complex sugars into simple, highly fermentable sugars, giving you a dry, thin beer.

## 4. LAUTERING: SEPARATING THE LIQUID AND SOLIDS

Lautering is the process of separating the sweet liquid — now called wort (rhymes with dirt) — from the grain husks and leftover fibrous materials.

The liquid part of the mash is drained off into a brewing kettle, and the grain matter remaining in the mash tun is rinsed with warm water, to further extract any additional sugar. As this process of rinsing, or 'sparging', continues, less and less sugar will be taken along with the rinse water. In the end, the brewer is left with a vessel full of sweet wort, and a mash tun of spent grain.

The wort is the beginnings of beer, and runs through the remaining processes. The spent grain waste has no real human nutritional value, but makes an excellent supplement to traditional animal feed. If you have a farmer friend, I'm sure they'd love to make use of your spent grain to feed their livestock!

## 5. BOILING THE WORT

The wort that resulted from the mash and sparge is collected in the brewing kettle, ready to be boiled.

Boiling the wort has a number of benefits.

Firstly, it helps to remove the excess and unwanted proteins that naturally exist in cereal grain. These proteins can have an undesired effect on beer presentation, by leaving it overly hazy.

Secondly, boiling sterilises the wort. Numerous strains of bacteria exist on grain. These bacteria are harmless to humans and don't warrant concern — they're the same or similar bacteria to that which exists on our skin, in our gut and all over most surfaces on Earth. But these bacteria will give our beer an undesired flavour, so to prevent this, we can kill off the bacteria by boiling the wort.

Thirdly, wort naturally contains a precursor to a flavour-negative compound called dimethyl sulfide. Thankfully, this particular compound is 'volatile', which means it can easily be driven off through a rigorous boil.

The final — and possibly most exciting — reason for boiling wort is to add bitterness, flavour and aroma to our beer through the addition of hops. Hops are the cone-shaped flowers of a tall bushy vine, which impart their different flavour attributes depending on what variety they are, and when they are added. They impart bitterness when added at the start of the boil, and they impart flavour and aroma when added to the end of the boil, where they spend relatively less time in contact with the hot wort. It's how we add our hops during this boiling process that determines if our beer is bitter, or if it just displays the aroma and flavour characteristics of the hop and is therefore simply 'hoppy'.

## 6. WHIRLPOOLING: CLEARING THE WORT

Once the boil is complete, there is a fair bit of coagulated proteins, called trub, and hop matter floating around in the boiled wort. Given enough time, these materials would all naturally settle to the bottom of the brewing kettle. However, as the wort slowly cools it becomes susceptible to bacterial contamination, undoing the sterilising effect of the boil.

> As brewers we are here, as we have been all along, to let nature do what it does best, all the while manipulating the conditions for the best possible flavour.

Thankfully, physics has provided a simple solution to this problem. With a minimal amount of mechanical input, brewers can encourage the separation of solids from the liquid. A current is started in the vessel, causing the liquid to swirl in a circular motion around the inside of the kettle. The result is a whirlpool, where the centrifugal force draws the liquid away from the centre of the vessel, pushing the liquid up against the walls. In doing this, the solids will be pushed to the centre of the vessel where they will settle as the current slows. The clear wort can then be removed by a syphon or drain from the side of the vessel.

Don't trust me? Sound too easy? I'll prove it. See Magic trick #1.

### 7. KNOCKING OUT — VERY COOL STUFF!

Once the whirlpooling is complete, we're ready to move our hot wort off our hops and trub, into the vessel in which it will be fermented.

During the whirlpool, the wort will have cooled slightly, but it's still far too hot to add, or 'pitch', our live yeast. In order not to kill the yeast, we have to cool the wort from near-boiling to yeast-pitching temperature as quickly as possible.

## Magic trick #1: Whirlpool in a glass

Go to the kitchen and grab yourself a wide, cylindrical glass and some oats or tea leaves (or any light material that will absorb water and then sink). Fill the glass with water to a reasonable distance from the top — you'll need to stir it, so don't fill it to the point it will overflow. Pour in a few grams, or a three-finger pinch, of the oats or other material and stir the glass to mix them, pushing down any floaters so they become wet. Wait a moment or two until the materials are hydrated, then give a consistent and gentle stir in a circular pattern around the glass. Only go in one direction. Once a good current is formed, remove your spoon and wait and watch. As the current slows to a halt, you will see the materials form in the centre of the glass. The wider and shallower the glass is, the more obvious the concentration of the materials in the middle will be. The success of this process is linked to a good, uninterrupted current, and not the speed of the current. The materials will stay in suspension until the current begins to slow.

Simply leaving wort to cool on its own is a risky proposition. Technically, in perfectly sterile conditions, it should work just fine — and it's the best use of natural resources as it requires almost no energy. So why not? The risk is that as the wort cools from a boiling temperature of 100°C (212°F) to a pitching temperature of 20°C (68°F), it travels through temperature zones where various bacteria are happiest. At this stage, our wort is loaded with nutrition for those bacteria and our yeast — and it's a race to see who gets in there and starts growing and eating first. We want our yeast to win, for the sake of flavour and all our effort to get to this point.

To give the yeast the best possible chance, we use refrigeration to achieve this temperature change. Through a piping system, or by putting the outside of the kettle in a bath of cooling medium, we're able to exchange heat from the boiled wort to the cooling medium. This process is very efficient and cools the wort at a controlled pace, making it ready for our yeast in a much shorter amount of time.

During this piping process we also introduce oxygen, a critical element in yeast growth. With well-oxygenated wort cooled to the right temperature, we're ready for the yeast, and for fermentation to begin.

## 8. FERMENTING

As brewers, we don't ferment anything — the yeast does all the work. We brewers are here, as we have been all along, to let nature do what it does best, all the while manipulating the conditions for the best possible flavour.

With our wort cooled and oxygenated in a sanitised fermenting vessel, we can now add, or 'pitch', our yeast.

Once the yeast has finished its job, our beer contains only a fraction of the sugar it began with, as well as alcohol, carbon dioxide and flavour compounds. It can be matured for a little or a long time, and will then be packaged as seen fit by the brewer.

Just prior to packaging, the beer will be 'conditioned' (a fancy word for carbonating, or adding carbon dioxide) to suit the brewer's intended flavour and texture, and their chosen packaging format, be it bottles, kegs or casks.

Enough work, now it's time for a beer!

# The yeast will go through a few phases...

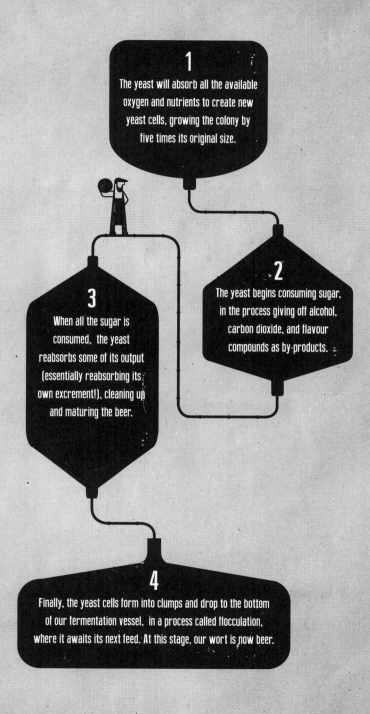

**1**
The yeast will absorb all the available oxygen and nutrients to create new yeast cells, growing the colony by five times its original size.

**2**
The yeast begins consuming sugar, in the process giving off alcohol, carbon dioxide, and flavour compounds as by-products.

**3**
When all the sugar is consumed, the yeast reabsorbs some of its output (essentially reabsorbing its own excrement!), cleaning up and maturing the beer.

**4**
Finally, the yeast cells form into clumps and drop to the bottom of our fermentation vessel, in a process called flocculation, where it awaits its next feed. At this stage, our wort is now beer.

# RAW MATERIALS

Chapter Three

Every beer you make tells a story. The raw materials you use say as much about you and your local beer culture as the finished beer itself. There are as many pale ales as there are brewers, and what will differentiate yours — beyond how well you brewed it — is why you chose to brew it, and why you selected the ingredients you used.

The quality of the beer begins with the raw materials. Bad raw materials — those that are out of date or haven't been stored properly — will make bad beer. Good raw materials — fresh hops for instance, packaged in appropriately sealed containers, and stored at the right temperature — are the basics for making good beer. The rest is up to you.

The core raw materials used in beer are malt, hops, yeast and water.

Other optional additional raw materials include fruits, herbs, spices, unmalted cereal grains, various forms of sugar, brewing aids, and indigenous bacteria and yeast.

## The big four

**MALT** gives beer its familiar sweet, bready, grainy flavour, as well as much of its texture. Malt provides the fuel for fermentation, essential nutrients for yeast, and proteins that create beer's characteristic foam.

Malt is the result of the malting process, during which a cereal grain (usually barley, but also wheat, rye and oats) is germinated and then dried, turning it from a nutrient-dense seed capable of being planted in the ground, into a form in which the seed's nutrients can be extracted by brewers for the purpose of fermentation.

**YEAST** makes beer. Brewers just make wort. The ebb and flow of any brewery is dictated by the yeast. A brewer's entire purpose is to create conditions where yeast is happy and comfortable — love your yeast, and those little critters will reward you with wonderful-tasting beer.

Yeast is a microorganism that consumes the fermentable sugars in wort, turning them into alcohol, giving off carbon dioxide, and giving you what we know as beer. Various strains of yeast have been selected by brewers and reused over the last few hundred years because of their pleasant flavours and ease of use. Today there are dozens, if not hundreds, of unique, commercially available varieties of brewers' yeast, each with their own unique flavour contributions and parameters for use.

The same malt and hop combinations, fermented with different strains of yeast, can taste as different as apple juice and coffee.

**HOPS** contribute bitterness to beer, provide flavour and aroma, and also have anti-microbial properties that help keep beer from spoiling. Hops are tall bushy vines, covered in cone-shaped flowers. It's the flowers of the hop plant that are used in the brewing process, as they contain highly prized oils. These oils break down in the brewing process, releasing their bitterness as well as their flavours, which range from grassy and spicy, to pine, citrus and tropical fruit.

**WATER** is one of the most vital compounds on Earth, and in its purest form has no real effect on beer flavour. However, all water supplies contain a certain level of minerals or chemicals that can, when found in high enough concentrations, define a beer style, or impart flavours and aromas to your beer — unwanted or otherwise. You can manipulate the flavour of water by removing or adding these chemical compounds and minerals to enhance a beer's flavour and replicate certain beer styles, or simply embrace the chemical signature of your local water to add uniqueness to your beer.

## Optional extras

**FRUITS, HERBS and SPICES** can elevate your beer's flavour and add colour, aroma and texture. In some beer styles, the addition of fruit and spices is essential to the flavour profile of the beer. Indigenous and wild fruits help brewers define the beer culture in their area, and help combat the effect of globalisation that makes products look and taste the same the world over.

**ADJUNCTS** are ingredients brewers add to boost certain elements of beer, like its alcohol level, body, and palate weight. They include unmalted versions of cereal grains like barley, wheat, rice, corn and oats, as well as various types of sugars. Some sugars will increase the sweetness and weight of beer and add another layer of flavour, while others are used for their thinning effects, and to provide more alcohol. Maple syrup, molasses and honey are also forms of sugar that we can use as adjuncts.

**BREWING AIDS** can help improve the look of a beer, help preserve the beer, and reduce brewing times. Some are naturally occurring compounds, and others are man-made, but none are essential. Some offer harmless boosts to your beer quality, such as yeast nutrients to boost the health of your yeast, and algae-derived additives that pull unwanted proteins from the wort, to improve its clarity. Others elicit extensive debate on what should and shouldn't be used in brewing — such as preservatives and antioxidants to prolong shelf life, chemical foam-control solutions to increase batch sizes and make more money, and clarifiers; all of these involve adding chemicals to do things that can otherwise be achieved through careful brewing practices and reasonable financial expectations, and some are also chemical versions of what can be achieved with natural additives. Each of these brewing aids contributes to the story of the beer you make, and should be carefully considered before using, and disclosed to the drinker.

The raw materials you choose — why you use them, how you use them and where you sourced them — all play into the story of each beer you make.

In the pages that follow we'll look at these in more detail, to help you understand the characteristics and effects of each raw material. Having a well-rounded knowledge of the raw ingredients available to you — as well as how to buy them, store them and use them — will enable you to create tasty, unique and personalised beers.

The same malt and hop combinations, fermented with different strains of yeast, can taste as different as apple juice and coffee.

# Malt

Malt is, by far, my favourite ingredient. Malt is a raw cereal grain that has been processed to chemically alter the starch-rich seed, making it ready to give up its fermentable contents. In commercial brewing, the brewer receives malt as a kernel. In home brewing you can also buy it as malt extract, in the form of a powder or syrup, where another brewer has already extracted the fermentable contents of the malt kernels so you don't have to.

When I began my beer explorations, before the craze of IPA, the most influential beers for me fell into the darker end of the style spectrum — brown ales and stouts — simply because these darker beers showcased the malt, by restraining the use of hops.

Malt and hops compete for your tastebuds, so by using fewer hops in the darker beers, the nuanced and varied malt flavours can be appreciated without distraction. Malt imparts a uniquely rich flavour which, when handled by a capable brewer, can give the perception of sweetness without the palate-fatiguing and belly-filling reality of actual sugar. Malt also has an elegant weight on the palate — something not found in many other beverages. And it can be quite varied in its flavour, depending on how it has been processed, and what grain type has been used.

## How malt is made

Malt can be made from many different cereal crops, including wheat, rye and oats — but more often than not, the term is used to refer to barley malt, and this is the type of malt I'll be referring to in this chapter.

Barley is unique in that it has a husk, which provides buoyancy in the mash tun, and acts as a filter bed when lautering (when the wort is drained off from the malt). Due to this natural filtration, barley is easier to process than other grains, making it the grain of choice for most brewers.

In a bid for innovation, less commonly used cereals like millet, sorghum, triticale and some native wild grasses are being commercially malted on a small scale. This is leading to new flavour experiences for beer drinkers, while at the same time opening a market for greater biodiversity in farming — helping to strengthen our food economy and regenerate our environment.

**A NOTE ON MALT EXTRACTS**
Malt extract is primarily derived from barley. With the increasing popularity of home brewing and the demand for other forms, suppliers have expanded to other cereal grains. Shop around and you'll find blends of wheat and barley extract, and maybe others. Malt extract producers still face the same processing issues as brewers, so you'll struggle to find 100% wheat or rye, but the percentages should be labelled on the packaging.

# Whole farm brewing: Be a farmer's friend

Farmers are business people. They take their cues from the market, and plant what people will buy. They have to weigh the input costs of a given crop, as well as its processing costs and distance to market, against the price they can get for it. If there's a market, and they can make money, they will grow it.

There are some conscientious farmers who will grow crops they can't harvest, simply for the sake of their soil. One way we as brewers can encourage more chemical-free or chemical-reduced soil management practices is to incorporate some of these nutrient-restorative grains like rye and oats into our brewing. Crop rotations are a proven land management technique that can improve soils without chemical inputs.

Buying the crops a farmer rotates in a paddock before or after planting their barley will encourage more farmers to practise these beneficial techniques. Not only that, these crops add complexity and flavour to your beer: a win–win.

To produce malt, the grain seeds are soaked in water to increase their moisture level from their dry state. This replicates the natural process that occurs when seeds are planted in the soil. In response to the elevated moisture level, the seed's naturally existing enzymes kick into action, converting its stored energy to a starch that can be accessed by a brewer — this is the beginning of the process we continue in our mash tun.

By utilising a tiny amount of this stored energy, the seed can begin to germinate, pushing out a rootlet. In the ground, this rootlet is searching for nutrients to feed the growing plant. In the malthouse, this rootlet serves as a visual indicator that it's time to stop the enzymes from converting all the starch to feed the growing plant — otherwise there'll be nothing left for us brewers!

To stop the enzyme activity, the sprouted, germinated grains are heated to dry them out. Initially, the temperatures are held relatively low to slow the enzymes without shocking them. As the enzymes are able to stand a higher level of heat, the temperatures are raised to drive flavour creation. At this point we have what's referred to as **pale malt** — the malt that makes up the vast majority of grain, by weight, used in making beer.

Alternatively, additional heat can be added to create a **kilned malt**, with a richer flavour.

Or the malt can be moved to a separate device with a more intense heat source, where it's roasted to drive even greater colour and flavour; these malts are appropriately named **roasted malt**.

A fourth category of malt, known as **crystal malt**, gets its signature look from a slightly different process. Rather than applying heat to drive off moisture, the malt is stewed in a sealed vessel. The moisture allows for further enzyme activity and conversion of starch into sugar within the kernel. The grain kernel, containing what is now liquid sugar, is then heated to crystallise the sugar, resulting in malt that has a glassy interior, is sweet to taste, and has had its starch fully converted to sugar.

## Base malts versus specialty malts

**Base malts** are the pale malt and kilned malts, and are the malts that provide the 'base' of any beer recipe. They make up the majority, by weight, of the malt used in a beer. They can be used in conjunction with other malts, or entirely by themselves. What makes base malts special is that they have sufficient enzyme levels, or 'diastatic power' (DP), to convert their starch in the mash tun. In fact, they have surplus diastatic power, and can also convert the starch in other malts that have little or no diastatic power.

**Specialty malts** are the roasted and crystal malts. These have little or no diastatic power, and therefore need to be used with base malt, which has surplus enzymes.

### PALE MALT IS PALE MALT IS PALE MALT, RIGHT?

No. Not all pale malts are created equal, and this variable can really throw off novice home brewers as they graduate into all-grain home brewing.

If you're just starting out and plan to use malt extract instead of grain, don't get overwhelmed or bogged down with this next section — just remember it's here for when you do try your hand at all-grain brewing.

The term 'pale malt' only refers to the style in which the grain was malted. When you read a recipe calling for pale malt, the author may have access to a malt that will yield a much sweeter beer than the one in your local home-brew shop. To truly understand what you can expect from the pale malt you're using, you need to know some key factors about the barley variety.

Different malthouses source different barley varieties, each of which has a different inherent diastatic power and other attributes — and even the same barley variety can change from year to year, and from paddock to paddock. This agricultural variability is something to embrace in your beer — the big side of town doesn't want to spend time and money adjusting to variation in their inputs, so they rely on a supply chain that delivers very uniform and consistent malt. This uniformity comes at a cost to the farmers involved and their land. They are beholden to this industrial supply chain and are price takers,

↑
Pale malt

meaning they can't afford to institute more environmentally sustainable farming practices due to the risk of variability of their output.

But when armed with a little understanding of malt and barley growing, we can adapt to what nature gives us and support those growers and maltsters who help us by farming sustainably, and reducing waste, pollution and greed in our supply chain.

Later on, we'll look at how to adjust your recipe and brewing process to adapt to the different pale malts you might have access to. For now, let me break it down two ways.

1. If you're brand new to brewing, you'll be using malt extract, and you'll have many more important variables to worry about than the variety of pale malt you're using. I'll tell you what to focus on when we actually get to making beer. Come back to this section when you've got a good grasp of the basics of the brewing process.

2. When you're ready to take on all-grain brewing, pick one manufacturer's pale malt that you have reliable access to, and use it in every beer you make — keep this variable constant as you focus on your process. As much as it pains me to say it, I suggest using a pale malt from a big, industrial malt provider, as they will have blended away any variability. Later on, when you've mastered the basics and are ready to tackle the challenge of adjusting your inputs, I highly suggest delving into the world of locally grown malt. The benefits to your beer flavour and story are worth the challenge.

## KILNED MALTS

These are classed as base malts, as they still retain enough 'diastatic power' through the kilning process to fully convert the starches in the grain. They can be used as 100% of the grist, or as a component of the total grist in conjunction with base malt.

Kilned malts come in various shades and flavour intensities. As the maltster increases the heat and processing time, and adjusts the humidity, the malt moves through the flavour spectrum, from the lighter **mild malt**, to **Vienna malt**, and the even richer, darker **Munich malt**. Some more intense kilned malts come with names like **aromatic** or **melanoidin malt**.

↑
Amber malt

↑
Chocolate malt

As you get to the darker end of the spectrum, you will want to reduce the percentage of that malt in your recipe. Melanoidin malt, for instance, falls out of the 'base malt' category and should be used with consideration to the manufacturer's recommendations.

Some newer companies — in an effort to differentiate themselves — have given unique brand names to malt products they've created using new techniques. This can make things a little tricky. Many smaller malthouses will post a chart on their website that suggests ways to substitute their malts for the more traditional malt varieties, so consult their websites and ask them questions about their malting methods. One such company is Gladfield in New Zealand.

**ROASTED MALTS**

When maltsters transfer the base malt to their roaster, they control the intensity of the roast through time, temperature and humidity — much like a coffee roaster. The result is a spectrum of malts from light to very dark, with an associated increase in the colour, and bitter (or 'acrid') flavour contributed.

From lightest to darkest, the roasted malts include:

- biscuit
- amber
- brown
- pale chocolate (not actually pale, but less roasted than full chocolate)
- chocolate
- roasted malt
- roasted barley.

↑
Dark crystal malt

↑
Light crystal malt

A mild roast flavour from a biscuit or amber malt gives an amber ale or lager a pleasant dry, roast character with a hint of colour.

As you move down the list and the roast gets more intense, the amount used needs to be considered. An overly dry beer with too much roasted malt can taste harsh and dusty on the palate — whereas residual sugar, detected on the palate as a malty sweetness, will help balance the bitterness of roast malt.

A pleasant coffee or chocolate flavour can be imparted when the more roasted chocolate and roasted malts are used in balance with the other flavours.

## CRYSTAL MALTS

Also known as 'cara' or 'caramel' malts, crystal malts have undergone extensive sugar conversion, or 'saccharification', in the grain kernel. The resulting sugar chains, known as dextrins, are small enough to not be classified as starch, but are long enough that yeast will not consume them. This means the sugar from this malt will make its way to your drinker's glass and will be a part of the taste experience. Dextrins add sweetness, palate weight and foam stability to your beer.

With today's modern barley being bred to have super-high diastatic power, for the most efficient production of alcohol — rather than with consideration to beer flavour — crystal malts have become an important contribution to modern beer. They put back the residual sweetness that has been bred out of some modern base malt. Plant breeders are making an effort to solve this flavour dilemma, but unfortunately plant breeding is very expensive and slow — and nearly all breeding projects are funded by private companies who service the very large industrial brewers. Those brewers are focused on making dry, easy-to-drink beers without much flavour. So home brewers and craft brewers who use the resulting industrial malt find the vast majority of the sugar from these barleys is consumed by the yeast, leaving a very dry, thin, and tasteless beer. The answer has been to restore some body, sweetness and flavour through the use of crystal malt.

Crystal malts are a perfectly good method of restoring or increasing body and residual sweetness to your beer, particularly when using malt extract with an unknown level of fermentability. They're easy to use, as they don't need to be mashed — but all this goodness doesn't come without a few negatives. Crystal malts oxidise relatively quickly, so should be used sparingly if shelf life is a consideration, as the more you use, the more oxidised flavour your beer will take on. Crystal malts also become overwhelming on the palate when used in too high a quantity. It's important to find the right balance with crystal malts, using as little as possible to ensure the best outcome for the greatest number of your beer drinkers.

An alternative way to restore body, sweetness and foam is to use a base malt that is less fermentable. We'll talk more about the specifics later.

## Other cereals

A few other very common malted cereal grains are also commercially available. Wheat is the most common and comes in the forms of pale wheat malt, dark kilned wheat malt, crystal wheat malt, roasted wheat malt and unmalted flaked wheat. Similarly, you'll find malted rye and crystal rye, as well as malted and unmalted/flaked oats.

Maltsters can apply the same techniques to most cereals, and what is commercially available is a result of demand from brewers.

**Wheat** gives beer a unique flavour and a soft, silky texture that's pleasant on the palate. It also contributes proteins, which have the positive effect of helping to contribute to strong, long-lasting and fluffy foam — which for me is the ultimate sign of a beer's quality — and the negative effect (if you're concerned with cosmetics) of beer haze, which has little or no flavour impact, but makes your beer appear cloudy. I feel the positives outweigh the negatives, and I use wheat in nearly every beer I brew. Because of wheat's lack of a husk, and its elevated levels of beta glucan (a gummy substance naturally existing in cereal grains), the lautering process is difficult, and many brewers use wheat to only half of their total grain component, even in beers marketed as 'wheat beer'.

**Rye** offers a unique flavour that's often referred to as spicy or earthy. Like wheat, it has a slightly different palate weight, offering a nice contrast to 100% barley beers. Also like wheat, rye has no husk, and with even more elevated beta glucan levels, can be even more

↑
Wheat

↑
Rye

challenging to process than wheat. My personal preference is to use no more than roughly 15% rye. At this level I achieve the desired rye character, without causing a 'stuck mash' and making my brewing day painfully long. Even at this level I'll add rice hulls — a food-processing waste product with no nutritional value. Rice hulls offer what the barley husk offers in terms of buoyancy and filtration, and can be sourced for relatively little cost.

Often described as silky and full, **oats** contribute many of the same attributes as wheat, but with their own flavour variation. Oats are most commonly available in unmalted, flaked form — the same as what you're used to eating for breakfast as oatmeal or porridge — but malted versions are also available. Like rye, oats should be used with consideration to lautering. They don't offer as much flavour as rye, so I wouldn't use more than 10% oats. (You can use up to 25–30% oats — I just don't know why you would!)

## Flaking it!

Flaking is a process whereby heat and moisture are applied to the grain before it is passed through rollers that compress it. The heat and moisture allow for some enzymatic activity to occur, and the rolling exposes the interior of the grain. Commercially available flaked grains include barley, oats, wheat, rye, rice and corn. All should be added directly to the mash as they will benefit from the clarification and surplus enzymes of barley for full saccharification (conversion of starch into sugars) and easy lautering.

A 'stuck mash' is when the mash tun output clogs up, and the wort stops running from the mash tun.

↑
Rolled or flaked oats

## One last word: buy local

By weight, malt is a much bigger raw material in beer production than hops, processing aids, and other adjuncts such as fruits and spices. It therefore is expensive to ship around.

Buy whatever malt you want. If you want to brew an authentic German pilsener, buy a German-made pilsener malt — but do so knowing that your malt took an awful lot of diesel fuel to reach you. Is it absolutely essential to you to have that German malt if you're in a country as far away as Australia? If you think the pleasure you'll get from the flavour that malt offers exceeds the environmental costs of drilling, refining and burning that fuel, then buy it.

Hopefully one day our collective consciences will move us, and our governments, to price these 'externalities' into our products, and we'll see the cost of malt produced on the other side of world exceed the cost of locally grown malt — thus rewarding our local producers and farmers, and encouraging us to buy these products that have used fewer non-renewable resources to arrive at our door.

The other aspect of the 'buy local' argument is around the celebration of the culture you're a part of. I live in Australia and I make Australian beer. The Germans make fine examples of beers using what they have local to them. As do the Americans, and many others. If I make beers that use their ingredients, in their styles, where would that leave Australian beer? Would there even be such a thing as Australian beer if we all replicate German and American beer?

I encourage you to learn to use the raw materials around you. Don't ask your growers and maltsters to change their product to replicate something grown elsewhere. Challenge yourself to produce something new and delicious, delighting your drinkers with the flavour you created from what you have locally available. When you buy local, and drink local, you experience the freshest quality of unadulterated beer that hasn't been scientifically engineered to travel great distances.

What you get is a pure representation of local beer culture, and an exceptionally satisfying beer experience.

# Good beer shouldn't cost the earth

With colourful labels and witty names, it's easy to forget that beer is actually an agricultural product, and that the beer you make or buy has had an impact on the environment throughout its production cycle. Hops and malt are the two main agricultural inputs in beer, and both are often treated as commodities, but they can vary as much as the beers made from them — not just in the flavours they create, but in how they were grown. And there are countless people involved in breeding, growing, transporting and malting the various cereal grains (barley, oats, wheat, rye) before we brewers get our hands on them. All of those people make decisions through their business practices about how much of an impact they're willing to have on our environment.

As a brewer buying malt, even on the relatively small home-brewer scale, we cast a vote for the farming and transport practices that get that malt to us. We get to brew beers that represent our values, and restore health to the environment and our local economy. When crafting our recipes, we get to ask ourselves, how far has that malt had to travel? Is it critical to our recipe to use malt transported from overseas — or is there a local replacement that depletes fewer natural resources, and still gives the resulting flavour we're after? Does the maltster buy from specific farms where she knows exactly how much chemical inputs are being used — or does she buy on the commodity market, where chemical-free farmers' barley is blended with conventional barley from all over?

Agricultural products can be produced in a way that restores the productive capacity of the earth, and as a brewer you get to choose suppliers who are supporting the farmers that are good stewards of the land, wanting to leave it fertile, healthy and chemical free.

# Hops

The world of hops is an ever expanding one. The innovation coming from the home brewing and craft brewing communities has led hop companies to push their breeding programs to new levels, turning out new varieties of tasty hops each year. To truly do these remarkable little flower buds justice you would need to dedicate an entire book to them — and thankfully people have.

However, my view is that all the fancy and expensive hops in the world can't make a poorly made beer taste good. Despite the fun you can have when experimenting with hops, my focus is to make sure you know how to use them in making clean-tasting, well-fermented beers. When you've mastered sanitation and fermentation, you'll have the skills to make beers that showcase these elegant, sticky nuggets of yellow lupulin goodness.

## What are hops?

Brewing uses the flowers of the female hop plant, where concentrations of bitter acids accumulate. These bitter acids are generally referred to as alpha acids. It's worth noting that there are other chemical compounds in hops that brewers analyse — but that's something to look into later in your brewing career.

Hop flowers, sometimes called cones, are picked from tall plants trained to trellises in vast commercial farms. The plants, called bines, grow to 4–5 metres (13–16 feet) in height. As the harvest season approaches, hop growers regularly analyse samples for their acid concentrations. When the plants have reached their target level of alpha acids, the madness of harvest kicks off. From the moment a plant reaches its desired alpha acid level, the race against time to pick, dry and package the hops begins.

Getting the hops into their vacuum-sealed packets in the shortest amount of time possible ensures they retain all their bittering, flavour and aroma characteristics. Hops are then stored cold, to slow their inevitable loss of potency.

# Why use hops?

Hops serve a few purposes in beer. The main one is to provide a sense of balance — their inherent bitter acids offset the sweetness of the malt. Without the bitterness of hops, the residual sweetness in beer (from the sugar not consumed by the yeast) is taxing to the palate. Beer's drinkability comes from the balance of the two, so as a brewer you need to always be aiming to find that balance. This requires constant consideration, because hops are an agricultural product — no two plants are identical, and the potency of each crop and hop variety will vary from year to year. Hops are packaged in such a way as to slow their deterioration, but nothing can stop it. That means we need to be conscious of what hop we're using in our beer, what level of acid it has, how old is it and how was it stored. I'll get back to these last three soon.

Hops also contribute to a beer's flavour and aroma. Traditional home-brewing texts have discussed flavour and aroma as two separate items, but the same principles apply to both, and they work hand in hand.

Hop's flavours and aromas are very complex. Earthy and spicy, citrus, tropical fruit, pine and candy are some of the descriptors for both flavour and aroma. Like many people, I sometimes struggle to define exactly which attribute I'm detecting — but I can always tell you if I like it! I think that's an important point. You'll never know what you get from a hop until you actually use it. The hop's marketing materials don't always make it clear what you'll get, and the ingredients you use it with may combine to produce something different than what you're told to expect. But that variety of flavour — and the pursuit of which combination of process and hop variety yields your desired result — is what makes hops such an exciting part of home brewing.

The final purpose of hops is to help stabilise your finished beer — minimising the change that occurs in your beer between when it is first made and when it is consumed. In particular, hops work by suppressing the growth of bacteria — the kind that will feed on your beer's residual sugar and in the process create flavours that don't taste good. This is the reason we have India Pale Ale today: by adding more hops, the beer

## Hop snapshot

**Saaz hops** (Old World, Czech): Elegant and gentle bittering; earthy, herbal and spicy flavour and aroma.

**Goldings hops** (Old World, English): Smooth, honey-like bittering; earthy flavour and aroma.

**Cascade hops** (American): Grapefruit and floral flavour and aroma.

**Nelson Sauvin hops** (New World): White wine and fresh gooseberry flavour and aroma.

**Galaxy hops** (New World): Tropical fruit and passionfruit flavour and aroma.

↑
Hop pellet

↑
Hop flower

could survive long sea journeys with its flavour still intact. The early brewers didn't know why the hops had that effect, but it worked — and that style of beer has lasted down the generations.

## Buying hops: flowers versus pellets

Hops come in two forms: flowers and pellets.

**Hop flowers** are less processed than pellets, but they're not as compact, so they require more space to store, and therefore cost more to ship. Some countries also have archaic rules around importing flowers — even though there is nothing fundamentally different between the flower and pellet. This makes hop flowers rare, and not worth you shopping for as they don't add any extra value when it comes to flavour. Some major brewers — who buy hops by the ton, and have appropriate cold storage and specially made brewing equipment — do claim the flowers result in a better flavour, but I'm not convinced. Regardless, as a home brewer, they will be hard to find — and even harder to find fresh and in good condition.

**Pellets** begin their life as flowers. They're ground up within hours of picking and pressed through a pelletiser, into tiny little cylinders about 6 mm (¼ inch) in diameter. This compressed shape makes them cheaper and easier to store and transport. Because of their ease of use, and the practically non-existent benefits of using flowers, pellets dominate the industry, and I won't spend much time talking about flowers.

# Hopping your brew: the 60-minute boil

Conventional home-brew hopping techniques from the 1990s and early 2000s involve adding your hops to your brew at different times during the boil, to achieve your desired outcome. Hops added at the beginning of the boil will add bitterness. Hops added toward the end will yield flavour. And hops added at the very end add aroma.

Hops require heat, through the action of boiling, to give up their alpha acids, and to bind those acids to the beer. Hops can also be added to fermented beer in a process known as 'dry hopping', for an additional hop aroma.

In a traditional **60 minute** home-brew boil, hop additions are referenced by the number of minutes remaining in the boil. The '60 minute' additions are the hops added when the boil starts. You set your timer for 60 minutes, and add your hops right away. These are the hops that will add bitterness and will be in contact with boiling wort for the full boil — and for some amount of time after the boil.

During this extended period two things happen. First, the hops' oils break down, releasing the alpha acids, which transform, or isomerise, into iso-alpha acid — the source of the bitter flavour of hops. The longer the hops are boiled, the more alpha acids are isomerised, and the more bitter the beer will taste. Second, the flavour and aroma compounds that are extremely volatile (or vaporous) are carried out of the solution through evaporation, caused by the vigour of the boil. This is the fundamental trade-off with all hops, and is very important when deciding on what hops to use and when. Hops with high alpha concentrations and less desirable flavour are excellent as bittering additions, because you don't need as much of them, saving you money — and you're not paying for a special flavour that will vaporise anyway!

As the clock ticks down to **30 minutes**, traditional hopping practices will have you adding your flavour hops. These hops will partially isomerise, and some of the aroma characteristics will be volatised (evaporated off) — but the dominant outcome will be the extraction of flavour.

As the clock ticks down to **5 minutes**, conventional practices will tell you it's time for your last hop addition. This one will have very limited contact with the boiling wort. In that time, the volatile aroma compounds will be extracted from the hops, but won't have been evaporated off. Flavour compounds will have begun being extracted, but only minimally. And very little, if any, isomerisation into bitter compounds will have had time to occur.

These traditional hop addition timings are still very accurate. Excellent beers showcasing good balance of malt and hop bitterness, with noticeable hop flavour and aroma, can be made like this. But don't fall into a trap of thinking you must add your hops at 60, 30 and 5 minutes — you can add your hops whenever you want. Like many things in brewing, the way you use hops is best visualised on a spectrum — in this case a spectrum of time in contact with the hot wort. The more contact time, the more bitterness, and as you reduce time you move through flavour and into aroma.

Some home-brewing techniques will have you leaving your hops in the brew kettle after the heat is turned off, at the expiration of the boil — referred to as **minute zero** of the wort boil, or 'flame out'. Regardless of what type of heat you use, be it a gas stove, electric stove or LPG camping burner, we still use 'flame out' to mark the end of the boil. But just because the heat is turned off does not mean the wort goes cold and the hops stop releasing their oils and isomerising their alpha acids.

At flame out, the brewer has two choices. One is to physically take the hops out of the boil kettle, if they were added in a way where this can be done. This will instantly stop the release of any more hop oils into the kettle — although the hot wort will still volatise and isomerise what's already in solution (more on that later).

The other is to use a whirlpool. This is used when hops have been freely added to the kettle to maximise their surface area with the hot wort and oil extraction; at flame out the hops are then separated from the wort by the magic of physics — which is how commercial breweries do it. This step, however, adds additional contact time with the hot wort, and impacts the timing of hop additions.

# New hopping methods

As home-brewing equipment has evolved to replicate the benefits of commercial equipment, hopping techniques have also evolved.

Amazing home-brewing innovation has occurred over the past 15 years, and drinkers' palates are changing and getting accustomed to hoppier beers. Because there are now so many more smaller and more localised breweries, their beers are being consumed closer to the source in shorter amounts of time while the hop flavours are still peak. To replicate what they are drinking fresh from their favourite local brewers, home brewers have been pushing innovation, and downsizing commercial equipment and processes to work in their home-brewing system.

The hop revolution is really what kicked off the craft beer revolution. Hops were traditionally grown as a commodity, and the varieties that held the highest concentration of alpha acids were the most valuable on the market. But those hops don't taste particularly interesting. The hop-growing industry responded very quickly to the demand of home brewers and craft brewers who have tossed out traditional hopping techniques in exchange for those yielding more flavour and aroma, without similar increases in bitterness.

The new Holy Grail in brewing is a beer loaded with hop flavour and aroma, with just a gentle bitterness to cut through the malt backbone. And the new Holy Grail for hop breeders is to produce a hop with excellent flavour and aroma, and not just high alpha acid levels.

Today's hopping techniques use greater quantities of hops than in the past, and focus the use of these increased quantities toward the end of the boil, after the boil (but before chilling), and after fermentation.

To mirror the results of commercial brewers, many home brewers have adjusted their techniques. Bitterness attained from a 60 minute addition can sometimes be too harsh, and bitterness from a much larger but later addition will add the benefit of flavour, while still allowing some isomerisation. Some modern aroma additions are even large enough to isomerise enough bitterness to achieve your balance without using a traditional 60 minute bittering addition at all.

The important take away here is that **hops can't read clocks**. So a 5 minute addition will not only add aroma, but also some flavour, and even some bitterness. Even if only a small percentage of your alpha acids isomerise in the aroma addition, you may still achieve your desired bitterness level if your addition is large enough. And to get the aroma people are chasing now, the aroma additions are huge!

## Fresh is best: be a hops fiend

As with most aspects of beer making and consumption, the freshness of your hops is critical. Hops degrade from the moment their acid levels peak while the flower is still on the bine. Processing them quickly into vacuum-sealed packages and storing them cold helps slow the degradation, but nothing stops it altogether.

Even when hops are added in beer, their flavour, aroma and bitterness degrade immediately. A beer consumed fresh will have noticeably more hop character than the same beer consumed even a few weeks later — especially if the brewer wasn't able or careful enough to keep out oxygen. So with hops, it's always a race against time, and a constant battle against heat and oxygen.

Most home-brew shops buy their hops in 5 kg (11 lb) packages. They then portion them down into the standard home-brewing sizes of roughly 100 g (3½ oz). This process exposes the hops to oxygen, an unfortunate reality.

When buying your hops, questions to consider are:
1. What crop year are they?
2. When did the home-brew shop open the bag?
3. Are the hops vacuumed sealed in their smaller containers?
4. Has the home-brew shop kept them cold?

You have to use what you have access to, but knowing how the hops were handled before you bought them will help you know if the flavour you're getting in your brew is the result of your process, or the quality of the raw materials. If the flavour of the hops you have access to isn't significant enough, use more next time.

> With hops, it's always a race against time, and a constant battle against heat and oxygen.

Prior to using your hops, visually inspect them. Knowing your hops will help you make adjustments on the fly that result in better beer.

- Are the pellets bright green? Or are they turning brown due to oxidation?
- Take a piece of a pellet and put it in the palm of your hand. With your thumb from your other hand, press the hop into your palm. Does it crumble right away, or is it dry and very hard? A fresher hop will break apart more easily.
- With your opposite thumb, rub the pellet into your palm in a circular motion. The friction and heat will help release the aroma, and the time it takes to break apart will help you gauge its freshness. If it takes ages to fall apart, this could indicate a hop that wasn't pelletised properly, and may not break down as easily when added to beer.
- Smell the hop in your hand. Record that smell memory in your brain, and remember it the next time you use the same hop. The more you smell, the more you have to compare to. If it doesn't smell as potent as last time, consider adding a little more.

↑
Hop pellet being crushed

## Expanding flavour horizons

While barley can be grown from the desert to the Arctic Circle and anywhere in between, hops cannot. Hops require a certain level of cold weather in winter, and extra hours of light in summer. This, coupled with adequate rainfall, will determine what regions will be successful for growing hops. Because of this, not everyone can buy hops from a farm nearby.

The American Prohibition of the early 20th century led to the failure of hop farms across most of the US, and the consolidation of the brewing industry. A couple of regions survived, and for years went unchallenged, as there wasn't enough demand for hops to warrant spending the money to convert lands back to growing them.

That has changed now and new entrants, attracted by high prices, are trialling plants in regions that haven't grown hops for years. With some fortitude and creative farming, we may see some new varieties that suit the climates of these more experimental regions, or some traditional varieties grown in these different climates may express themselves in new ways, offering brewers even more flavours to experiment with.

Exciting times are ahead regardless, and opportunities to make truly local beers using hops and malt from your region make it exciting to travel and explore new beer cultures.

By reducing our beer miles to the absolute minimum, we can drive innovation and outpace the effects of globalisation — and truly celebrate what makes each beer region in the world unique.

# Keeping it real

There is a danger that the success of craft beer brands will lead to more consolidation across the world, and a sterilisation of local beer cultures. As the big mega brewers absorb small brands and ship them around the world, they displace the local beers due to their price point and reputation. If this goes unchecked, every city you visit will have the same beers on offer and the unique craft beers will evaporate. Home brewing kicked off this great beer revolution we're currently in, and I believe it will be the factor that keeps the big brewers at bay.

Small-scale, regional beer production — where malt and hops don't travel great distances to breweries to be converted into beer, and where the beer is consumed close to the brewery — can have a major impact on what our planet and our economies look like in the future. By crafting beers at home, we take this movement to the next level: the beer may not even leave the house! And we can choose to support people in the supply chain who do things that are right for our world.

# Yeast

There is an adage that says 'brewers don't make beer, yeast does' — which is partly what makes yeast so fascinating.

Sure, brewers create a nutritious environment for yeast to thrive in, and give them a nice clean home maintained at just the right temperature — but the yeast does all the work when it comes to creating texture and flavour in beer.

## It's a living thing!

Yeast is a living organism that feeds on the sugar within wort, converting it to carbon dioxide, alcohol and flavour compounds — which is the actual process by which beer is made. And its flavour impact is incredibly varied. Relative to the more obvious effects of malt and hops, yeast has an outsized impact on the final taste, as using different yeast strains can make the same brew taste entirely different.

What also makes yeast so cool is how it has evolved, thanks to the generations of brewers who have been looking after it for the hundreds of years we've been making and enjoying beer. Early brewers would have noticed the sludge in the bottom of a fermenting vessel, and I imagine they understood it was a crucial part of the brewing

↑
Dried yeast being rehydrated

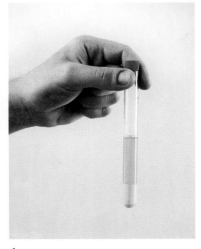

↑
Liquid yeast in a sample of beer

process. But it wasn't until the advent of the microscope that yeast was actually identified.

Yeast exists naturally nearly everywhere in the world, and most of it is not useful for making good beer — brewers through the ages have selected the right type of yeasts to give us beers we enjoy today.

Early beers would have tasted quite earthy, sour and rough. The earliest brewers would have decided to reuse certain fermenting vessels, using the same yeast, because the flavour from the last batch was better than in other batches. The yeast from the bad batches would have been discarded, and the yeast that naturally made good-tasting beer would have survived and been reused and carried forward for future brewers to use — a process of natural selection.

The evolution of yeast is entirely linked to human evolution. Modern brewer's yeast has mutated and evolved through the nurturing of brewers over generations to the point where it's no longer comparable to its wild brethren. The yeast cells that performed well in the conditions brewers set were reused, and future generations of those particular yeast organisms would have developed to function in the environment in which they were created. Just as a newborn calf set loose in the wild wouldn't survive, neither would domesticated brewer's yeast.

Yeast is one of the many parts of brewing you can easily become obsessed with, but for now I'll stick to discussing the world of commercially available brewer's yeast. Some exceptionally complex and flavoursome beers are being made from wild yeast found on fruit, flowers and in the air, but these beers take skills beyond the scope of this book.

**Yeast exists naturally nearly everywhere in the world, and most of it is not useful for making good beer — brewers through the ages have selected the right type of yeasts to give us beers we enjoy today.**

## Domestic brewer's yeast: banking on it

The commercial landscape of brewing has led to the development of yeast banks. When a consumer enjoys a beer and wants to buy it again, they expect it to taste the same. However, because yeast is a live organism, it can reproduce every 3–5 days, meaning it can evolve (or mutate) quickly. If this mutation were to go on unchecked, the beer you drink from your favourite brewery six months later would taste different than the last time you tried it.

To keep this mutation in check, yeast banks will cryogenically store parent cells of yeast, from which they can restart new batches (or 'cultures') of yeast for the brewers they work with. This means that brewers can start with a fresh batch of yeast, with the same genetic material as their favoured yeast, whenever they feel their yeast's performance is faltering, and beer flavour is starting to drift.

As a home brewer, you have access to the same strains of yeast from these yeast banks. They package and sell small-scale versions, sized to ferment the standard 19 litre (5 gallon) home brew batch.

Yeast comes in two forms: a dried powder and liquid. Both have their benefits and drawbacks, and both are perfectly acceptable.

## Dried versus liquid yeast

**Dried yeast** is alive, but in a dormant state. It can stay like this for a very long time. However, the longer it is dormant, the fewer cells will likely come out of hibernation, so there is a limit to its shelf life — but it lasts much longer than liquid yeast. Because it has been dried, it also takes up far less space, making it easier to ship. With their relatively long shelf life and ease of transport, dried yeast packets are reasonably inexpensive compared to liquid. They are good value and I highly recommend them, particularly when you're starting out — using a packet of dried yeast batch after batch will help reduce the number of variables you have to deal with, helping you master your brewing process.

**You'll find a wider variety of yeast strains in liquid form. At the time of writing this book, one dried yeast manufacturer offered 12 varieties of yeast, while a well-known liquid yeast provider offered 58 strains.**

↑
Commercial examples of liquid (left) and dried yeast (right)

**Liquid yeast** is alive and awake — or perhaps better described as napping (rather than hibernating, like dried yeast). It has been grown from a single parent cell to a size that is almost ready to ferment your 19 litre (5 gallon) batch. It comes in either a package with some storage solution, or a 'smack pack' with a small amount of food to munch on after its nap. Both forms serve the same purpose: to protect the yeast during its journey to you. Transporters who leave it in a hot truck or on your front verandah in the sun inadvertently harm the yeast.

## A yeast for every brew

Yeast varieties refer to the style of beers the unique yeast strains make. Beer styles, as we learned earlier, can be defined by their colour, sweetness, hop presence, and yeast flavour. Two different yeast strains can make the same wort taste completely different.

Some varieties are preferred as they are more forgiving of sudden changes in temperature, which is good for home brewers with little or no temperature control, while other yeasts will give up and stop fermenting at the slightest hint of any change in their conditions.

Some create massive, bold flavour compounds, called phenols, which taste like pepper and cloves, while others are used for their neutral taste, which doesn't interfere with the coveted hop flavours.

## Ale yeasts versus lager yeasts

As we saw earlier, in the hierarchy of beer styles, a beer is either an ale or a lager, and it's the yeast that determines this classification.

Yeast is alive, and like us, responds to temperature. Generally speaking, ale yeasts and lager yeasts are categorised based on their preference to operate in a relatively warm (ale) or cool (lager) environment. When warm, yeast operates quickly and releases a greater amount, and higher intensity, of flavour compounds.

## ALE YEASTS: QUICK AND DIRTY

Ale yeasts are like the food truck chef who makes the perfect bacon cheeseburger. The van is parked out in the sun, turning out superfast burgers, dripping with grease and cheese, reeking of fried potatoes, sweat dripping down the faces of cooks frantically keeping up with their orders. The output has big and bold flavours, tastes great, but there's grease on the walls and the grill needs to be scraped clean.

At fermentation temperatures of 17–25°C (63–77°F), ale yeasts work quickly to ferment and mature the beer, and finish their work in 5–10 days. When chilled, the yeast responds quickly to the temperature change and the cells 'flocculate' (clump together) and drop out of suspension, ready to ferment their next batch.

## LAGER YEASTS: CALM, COOL AND REFINED

Lager yeasts are like the white-tablecloth restaurant chef who finishes her shift with not a spot on her whites. She turns out meticulous dishes, with every morsel precisely cooked and plated. She works over a long shift, at a deliberate pace, to create precise and clean flavours. The output is nuanced, refined and balanced, and the lack of bold flavours means every element can be appreciated.

At a fermentation temperature of 10–14°C (50–57°F), the yeast performs slowly, consumes sugar more slowly, and in the process produces fewer flavour-negative compounds. Lager yeasts also continue to operate at very low temperatures of 0°C (32°F) or below — temperatures where haze particles drop out of suspension, but where yeast can continue to absorb flavour-negative compounds, cleaning up the beer to produce a vibrant, clean, bright flavour. This is best done in a horizontal lager tank, where the surface area of the sedimented yeast

| A typical ALE ferment in a commercial brewery | A typical LAGER ferment in a commercial brewery |
| --- | --- |
| Initial fermentation temperature: 19°C (66°F) for 4–5 days | Initial fermentation temperature: 10°C (50°F) for 10–12 days |
| Fermentation clean-up: 21°C (70°F) for 2 days | Fermentation clean-up: 16°C (61°F) for 4–5 days |
| Maturation: as close to 0°C (32°F) as possible for 5–7 days | Maturation: as close to 0°C (32°F) as possible for 20–30 days |

is greatest, maximising contact with the beer. In a vertical maturation vessel, such as a home-brew fermenter, this will still happen, but will take more time.

## Yeast: delving deeper

When the time comes to explore other yeast varieties and the styles of beer they make, here are the attributes you'll need to consider.

### FLAVOUR: WILL IT HAVE ANY?

This speaks to whether the yeast is neutral, or whether it produces a high level of phenols and esters (compounds that yield flavour). The nuance of phenols and esters is a bit complicated, so it's sufficient to know that they exist, and are responsible for the spicy and fruity aromas in your beer.

Production of these flavour compounds varies by yeast strain, and some produce levels that are below what most people can taste — which would be considered fairly neutral yeasts.

Others, like some of the Belgian and German strains, are selected for their high levels of esters and phenols, and the flavours they impart when combined with the other ingredients in the beer.

The German hefeweizen yeast is famous for its banana (ester) and clove (phenol) flavours, while the Belgians have saison and wit strains that are equally expressive, offering earthy, peppery and spicy flavours.

**ATTENUATION: HOW MUCH SUGAR WILL IT DEVOUR?**
Technically speaking, attenuation is the measure of sugar consumed by the yeast. Because sugar plays an important role in the flavour and texture of the finished beer, a yeast strain's expected attenuation will heavily affect the final flavour — and needs to be considered in the recipe from the start.

Unfortunately, attenuation is also heavily impacted by many aspects of how the beer is made, so manufacturers can't assign a meaningful attenuation number to each strain of yeast. They can only offer relative terms like 'high', 'moderate' or 'low', and it's up to brewers to experiment, know their system and what results they've achieved in the past, so they can make their own judgment of what the yeast will do for them.

**OPTIMAL OPERATING TEMPERATURE**
As we've discussed, yeast is very temperature sensitive, and each strain has its own optimum temperature range. When starting out, you won't have great (if any) temperature control, and this will be one of your biggest challenges to making a consistent, deliberate flavour (if this is what you're after, of course).

If you don't have good temperature control, this also limits your choice of yeast strains. If your house gets cold in winter, that's a great time to try brewing a lager, or a beer that uses a yeast that benefits from a long, cool maturation, like a German altbier or kölsch.

## Buying yeast

Yeast stored improperly — for example, unrefrigerated, or for too long past its expiry date — will not make good beer. There are relatively few yeast providers, so it may be difficult to support a local one — instead, I suggest you find a local home-brew shop (or an online store) that buys yeast frequently, stores it in a fridge, and ships it to you with ice or in a cool pack. Develop a relationship with the staff and learn when they order yeast. If you have a specific strain you'd like to try, ask them to order it for you, and plan your brewing schedule around its expected arrival so it's used as soon as possible.

Home-brew shops will store more of the yeast strains they sell frequently, but they should be happy to order you something if you're willing to work into their ordering schedule.

**REMEMBER, KEEP IT COLD!**
Keep your yeast in the fridge, and don't buy from anyone who doesn't. Yeast is alive, and will stay happiest when stored cold. Don't test this, it's not a theory! Keep it cold.

Just as a newborn calf set loose in the wild wouldn't survive, neither would domesticated brewer's yeast.

# Magic trick #2: Keep it simple

For your first few batches of beer — while you work out your process and understand the flavour you get from your choice of malt extract — stick with a dried ale yeast strain.

Most companies will offer two ale yeasts: an American Ale and an English Ale. The American Ale favours a ferment temperature of 18–19°C (64–66°F), while the English Ale prefers a slightly warmer temperature of 20–21°C (68–70°F). The American variety is relatively more neutral in flavour, while the English variety will consume less of the malt sugar, resulting in a slightly sweeter beer.

By brewing with the same yeast in your first few batches, you're limiting the variables that can impact the flavour. If your yeast doesn't 'attenuate' (consume as much sugar) as you'd like, and you changed the malt and the yeast from batch to batch, how will you know which variable affected the outcome — or how much change is attributable to each variable? Find out by changing just one variable at a time.

# Water

Water is one of the four core ingredients in beer. You can't make great beer with bad water, but your water doesn't have to be fresh from a mountain spring, either. When you've tackled the other brewing issues and you still want to improve your beer — you should never stop trying to improve your beer! — then look to adjusting your water.

So how do you know if your water is 'bad'? There are kits you can buy to test for mineral content, or you can go online and check your water company's tolerances for each mineral. But before you spend time doing this, check out the tip below.

For your first few brews, use cold water from your tap. Don't use your garden hose, as the materials the water travels through will impart flavour into your water.

If, after the first batch, you find the taste of your water still makes it into your beer, and you don't like it, you can try the following options.

1. **Buy bottled water** – this is costly and involves a fair bit of plastic to recycle, but the flavour of the water will be a known quantity. The water will be clean and should be free of excessive minerals and chlorine.
2. **Use a filter** – you can buy decent carbon filters, for chlorine and chloramine, at most hardware stores.

Chances are, if your water is so loaded with chemicals that you don't want to brew with it, then you'd probably benefit from installing one anyway, so you can enjoy drinking your tap water.

3. **Camden tablets** – these are an easily dosed quantity of sodium metabisulfite, which reacts with chlorine, eliminating its negative downstream aroma contributions. The drawback is that they are a sulfite, which some people are sensitive or even allergic to. I'm not qualified to confirm whether or not detectable concentrations will carry through into your finished beer; please do your own research and make your own informed decision.

If your water has an especially high mineral content, you can soften it by boiling your water the day before and letting it cool. Some of the minerals will precipitate out of solution, leaving a white powder on the bottom of the pot. Drain the water into a new pot, leaving the white powder behind, then brew away. The downside of doing this is the energy expense, the need for a very large pot, and the time and planning required — so you'll have to decide for yourself how important it is to remove the water's flavour from your beer.

## Before you splash out: Pour yourself a glass

Turn on the tap and pour yourself a glass of water. Look at it: is it clear, or does it have a tint? Taste it: does it have a mineral weight, and can you taste chlorine? As a beginner home brewer, if you drink your own tap water you probably won't mind drinking beer made from it. If there is a hint of chlorine, don't worry too much; most of it will be boiled off. And if it has a slight minerality, don't stress — some regions of the world are famous for producing certain beer styles that suit the water they have access to. The mineral content of your water may affect your ability to produce a perfect Pilsner, but I'm confident you'll still be able to make a very enjoyable lager. I've been blessed with excellent water in all of the locations I've brewed in, both at home and commercially, so admittedly I'm not a water expert — but I've always looked to make 'my' beer with what is available to me, including water.

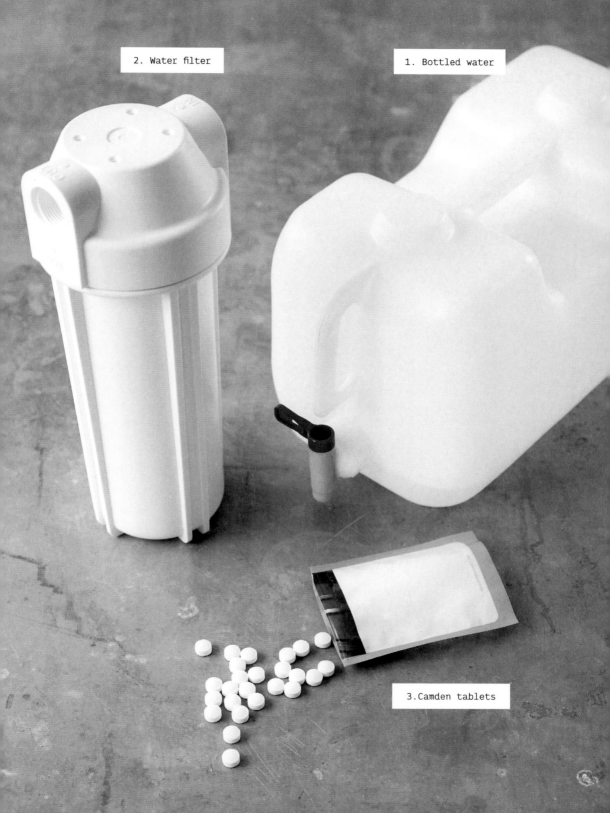

2. Water filter

1. Bottled water

3. Camden tablets

# Other ingredients

We've now looked at the four core ingredients in beer — malt, hops, yeast, and water. Other optional raw materials include various forms of sugar, fruits, herbs, spices, processing aids, and indigenous bacteria and yeast.

## Adjuncts: other fermentable sugars

In industrial brewing, adjuncts are sources of sugar that are cheaper and more fermentable than malt; these are used because they are the most efficient source of alcohol. They also serve the purpose of thinning the beer, to make it palatable to more people. An all-malt beer will have a certain amount of unfermented, or residual, sugar that some consumers find heavy or too full-flavoured. By replacing some of the malt with a more highly fermentable adjunct, the beer will offend fewer people — and bore more people.

As home brewers, we have access to many of the same adjuncts as industrial brewers, but we tend not to use them for exactly the same reason commercial brewers do — we're trying to make interesting, full-flavoured beers. In the home-brew setting, an adjunct that thins our beer would generally have no place, but there are some adjuncts that boost flavour and offer processing assistance without dumbing down our beer — primarily corn sugar (dextrose) and milk sugar (lactose).

### DEXTROSE FOR BOOSTING ALCOHOL

Dextrose, or corn sugar, is a highly fermentable sugar that raises the alcohol in those beers where adding more malt to achieve the desired lift in alcohol level would make the beer too full-bodied. At the higher end of the alcohol scale, say 7% or more, an all-malt beer will have a fair bit of residual sugar. When brewers want to increase the alcohol level of a beer, without the extra residual sugar malt would contribute, they can turn to dextrose instead. Rather than thinning a 4.5% pale ale, turning a balanced beer into a thin beer, adding dextrose instead of more malt will keep a heavy beer from crossing into an unpalatably heavy one.

Whereas malt extract ferments only 70–85%, dextrose ferments completely, in a clean manner, with no flavour additions. However, when used in high quantities, it will lead to noticeable thinning of the beer, which will impact flavour.

**LACTOSE FOR 'CREAMINESS'**

Lactose is unfermentable, meaning that as a molecule it's too complex for yeast to consume, and offers a very different palate weight to malt. Lactose leads to a creamy texture and is the key ingredient in milk stout. As it is unfermentable, 100% of its sugar will end up as residual sweetness in the beer, so use it cautiously — too much residual sweetness will limit the enjoyment of your beer.

## Processing aids

My goal has always been to make minimally processed beer.

'Processing', as I'm referring to it, can be mechanical — like filtering out yeast and particles to clarify the beer — or can involve adding an ingredient that causes a desired reaction. Processing is not inherently bad, but each method has its own costs and benefits to consider. It all comes down to what your values and priorities are.

Beer clarity is a very relevant example. Do you drink with your eyes and want your beer to be crystal clear? Or do you appreciate the fact that, in its natural state, a beer made with flavour as the number-one priority might be slightly cloudy?

Since the advent of clear glass drinking vessels, beer has been judged on its appearance. Back in time, haze in beer implied it was hastily made, or had bacterial contamination. The way to make a clear beer was to ferment it well in a sanitary way, and give it the time it needed to 'drop bright' — when particles and yeast fall to the bottom of the vessel, leaving the beer bright and clear. In a commercial brewery, maturation time is the enemy of economic gain, so processes of removing the yeast and particles were invented. With these, bright beer could be created faster, giving the illusion of a properly aged and well-made beer, with all the cost savings of a quickly produced beer. However, while filtering satisfied a cosmetic and commercial need, it did nothing for flavour.

It's similar to what has happened in the fresh food world, with the consumer having been trained to want only perfectly shaped

I use lactose in a coconut pale ale at a rate of roughly 3% by weight of the grain (in a 21 litre/5½ gallon home brew I suggest you start by adding 100 g/3½ oz), and it adds a touch of creaminess to enhance the flavour of the coconut. And in a milk stout, where lactose is one of the key components, I use it at a rate of roughly 10% of the weight of the grain (about 450 g/1 lb for a 21 litre/5½ gallon 4.4% ABV home brew). At that rate it plays a crucial role, adding sweetness to balance the bitterness of the roasted malt.

produce. I know a market gardener who has a 90/10 rule: 90% of a bundle of her produce needs to be blemish free, and 10% can have a blemish, provided it doesn't detract from flavour. When you become a home brewer, like a gardener, you need to toss aside these ideas that marketing companies have placed in our heads about what makes food and beer taste good. A carrot shaped like the letter 'C' doesn't taste any worse than a straight one — and a hazy pale ale brewed 15 days ago, loaded with fresh hop character, tastes way better than one that was processed to be brilliantly clear in an effort to prolong its shelf life.

In the home-brew setting, I see no benefit in messing around with a risky process for the benefit of touching up the cosmetics of my beer if it doesn't add to the flavour — and the risk of making the beer worse greatly outweighs the benefits. That being said, there are some inexpensive processing aids we can use that have little or no negative effects. As a home brewer, kettle finings and yeast nutrients are two you can consider (see below). There are others you can use, such as anti-foam (a.k.a. foam control), commercial enzymes and preservatives — it just comes down to what you want your beer to stand for.

## KETTLE FININGS

Also known as 'copper finings', these are added during the boil. They interact with excessive proteins, causing them to clump together, forming a mass that drops to the bottom of your brewing kettle by gravity or in the whirlpool. In the past they have been made from unsustainable sources (such as fish bladders), but modern kettle finings are derived from algae and are vegan friendly. They will not make your beer crystal clear, but do slightly take the edge off a haze, with no negative effects on flavour.

## YEAST NUTRIENTS

These are like a multivitamin for your yeast. They act as a supplement to boost the nutrient levels naturally existing in the malt, so the yeast has all the nutrition it needs. In the event your yeast needs a little help, these nutrients will ensure a full and healthy ferment, and the yeast

can be used to ferment another batch. If your malt has everything your yeast needs, adding yeast nutrients will be waste — but it won't make your beer any worse. Think of it as insurance.

## Fruits, herbs and spices

Fruit has been used in beers for hundreds of years. I'm sure some brewers have used fruit to cover a few flaws in fermentation, particularly before brewing science discovered yeast and understood fermentation.

Fruit can also be used to enhance the flavour and visual appearance of beer. Berries and stone fruit are excellent beer companions. Citrus, particularly citrus peel, can be a great addition when used sparingly.

Spices such as coriander seeds play a pivotal role in building the flavour profile of some beer styles. Traditional Belgian witbiers, such as Hoegaarden, use coriander seed and Curaçao, the peel of a bitter orange the Dutch imported from the Caribbean.

Experimentation is needed to balance spice into the flavour of the beer you're brewing, but if you are familiar with how spices are used in cooking, and factor in the effects from fermentation and aging on those flavours, you have a leg up on figuring out how to use almost any spice you enjoy to enhance a beer.

# *Don't try this at home: A vanilla disaster!*

In one of our brews, in an effort to be natural and authentic, we rejected using vanilla extract in favour of real vanilla beans. We meticulously sourced hundreds of these finicky pods, then spent hours splitting them all in half and scraping out all the tiny seeds. We then gleefully added the vanilla seeds to the kettle and were so impressed with ourselves as the vanilla aroma filled the brewery. We'd nailed it!

We 'knocked' the beer out to the fermenter and pitched our yeast, and again were pleased to see an active and vigorous ferment start up shortly after. Remember, in the fermenter, yeast activity is causing churning, and the production of carbon dioxide carries (usually negative) flavours out of the beer.

Whatever vanilla hadn't been flashed off (or volatised) in the boil of the kettle, had been obliterated in the ferment. The finished beer had no trace of vanilla!

# Small beer: putting the world to rights

As you may have guessed by now, one of my motivations for writing this book is to open a conversation on the consequences of the current industrial food system, which beer is a part of.

We live in a world food economy that, despite its noble intentions of feeding a growing population, has evolved into something that benefits the few, at the expense of the many. Farmers are paid rock-bottom wages to supply the industrial system with cheap raw materials, farmed in a way that damages our environment. Soils become more and more nutrient depleted as chemical-dependent plants yield food with bland or no flavour, without anything of value going back into the soil. These bland raw materials are sent on a massive scale to industrial brewers, who manufacture and distribute mass-produced beer with no regard for the cultural and environmental destruction being caused.

Mass production leads to globalisation and the suppression of 'local' cultures. When something like Bud Light becomes available in every city in the world, the local beer culture is displaced because the smaller, local producers can't compete with a multinational's artificially low production costs.

But there are alternatives. There is a vibrant farming community ready to service your brewing needs. Through the purchase decisions we make, we have the ability to change our economy and environment for the better. I source my materials carefully, and by supporting producers on the same journey as me, I have access to a greater variety of more flavourful and sustainably produced ingredients. At times it does cost more for some of these inputs, but often times it doesn't — malt is heavy, and fuel is expensive, so by buying local and shortening the distance our inputs travel, we benefit the environment and our bottom line.

I'd love you to embrace brewing with the same ethos, as much as possible.

# EQUIPMENT

## Chapter Four

If you've skipped the last few chapters because you just can't wait to get fermenting, I don't blame you. I did the same when reading my first brewing book. So enough theory and raw materials — let's get into the guts of it.

# Your home brewery

Your brewery may not look like a commercial brewery, but it's still a brewery. You will perform many of the brewing tasks commercial brewers do, using the equipment you can access and in the space you have — and you don't need much space or equipment to get started.

**BESIDES YOUR BASIC KIT, ALL YOU'LL REALLY NEED IS:**

- a sink, to wash your kit and cool your wort
- a heat source — your domestic gas or electric stove is perfect
- a bench or counter to rest your equipment on
- a clean, dry, temperature-stable area to ferment in.

Even the smallest of apartments, provided you have a forgiving partner or housemates, can accommodate your home brewery.

Most home-brew shops will stock everything you need, but don't rush out and buy anything if you already have something that's reasonably similar. For example, your pasta strainer is the perfect tool for rinsing your grains after you steep them in the kettle — so don't go and buy something marketed to home brewers that does the same thing. Some of the more generic items you can find cheaper at a kitchen store or hardware store: instead of a thermometer marketed for home brewing, you can use your standard meat thermometer, provided you can adequately clean and sterilise it. Work within your budget, whatever that that may be.

To know what equipment you'll need, you need to know a little about what you'll be doing. Let's run through the various methods of home brewing, from easiest to most difficult.

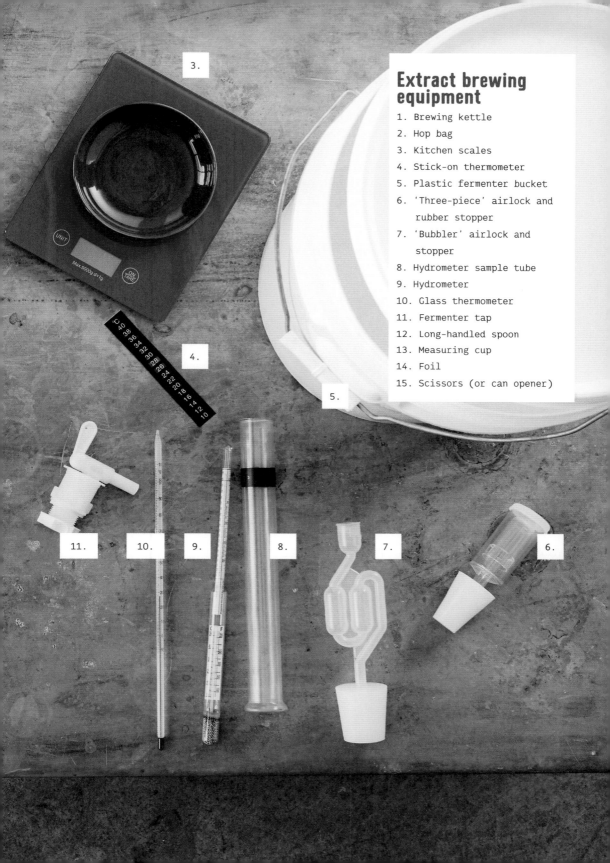

**Extract brewing equipment**

1. Brewing kettle
2. Hop bag
3. Kitchen scales
4. Stick-on thermometer
5. Plastic fermenter bucket
6. 'Three-piece' airlock and rubber stopper
7. 'Bubbler' airlock and stopper
8. Hydrometer sample tube
9. Hydrometer
10. Glass thermometer
11. Fermenter tap
12. Long-handled spoon
13. Measuring cup
14. Foil
15. Scissors (or can opener)

# 'No Boil' or 'Kit and a Kilo' brewing

This is the most basic method of home brewing — and it's one I hope you all skip. In this 'instant coffee' version of home brewing, you buy a 'kit' (a tin of malt extract) and a kilo of sugar and add both straight into a sanitised fermentation vessel with water and yeast. Your interaction with the brewing process barely exists in this method, and you have very limited input into the flavour you're creating.

You don't get to pick your hops and customise your flavour and aroma. You also don't get the benefit of a boil in driving off chlorine and removing the excess protein through 'trub' creation.

You don't learn to cool and aerate your wort, and you don't get to appreciate the wonderful smells, the creative release and the camaraderie of home brewing.

For me, the joy is not just in sharing and drinking the beer, though that is fun — it's the process of making it. With this method, you learn very little that you can build on to grow as a brewer and create better-tasting and more varied beers.

Cutting corners will just hold you back, so don't get off on the wrong foot. Skip this method of brewing and never look back.

# Method #1: Extract brewing

This form of brewing is simple and involves a reasonably small amount of money, time and equipment — and is the perfect method for your first batch.

While you're not starting with the raw grain, as a commercial brewer would, you're boiling your wort to enhance flavour, and setting the stage to focus on the two most important aspects of brewing: sanitation and fermentation.

With this method of brewing we get our fermentable sugar from malt extract, either dried as a powder, or in syrup form. This is added to hot water and brought to a boil. Hops are also added, based on the recipe. The boiled wort is cooled, aerated and added to a clean and sanitised fermentation vessel. The yeast is pitched and fermentation is monitored.

There are two main downsides to this brewing method. The first is that malt extract is meant as a base, and tends to only come as 'light', 'medium', 'dark', or as a 'wheat' version. The second is that malt extract can lead to a thin-tasting beer, because the amount to which it will ferment — its attenuation level — is 'baked in' by whoever made it, and it's something they can rarely, if ever, tell you. So you won't know if your beer will be full with a big mouthfeel, or more likely thin and watery.

But this is an okay method for your first batch. When you're ready to try a wider selection of beer styles, you can move on to the 'extract plus specialty grains' section further in the chapter.

# Extract brewing: tools of the trade

### 15 LITRE (4 GALLON) BREWING KETTLE (ENAMEL COATED OR STAINLESS STEEL)

- In extract brewing, we're not doing a full wort boil. Instead, we're making a concentrated ('high gravity') wort, and watering it down to brewing strength in the fermentation vessel. This means you can brew using a domestic gas or electric kitchen stove.
- You can just use a great big stockpot as your brewing kettle. Stainless steel is the best option, but an enamel-coated pot is also good, and five times less expensive.

### LONG-HANDLED SPOON

- Stainless steel is ideal because it won't take on or leach flavours, nor will it rust. It's also easy to clean and sanitise. A food-grade plastic spoon will do, but it can take on other flavours, so don't use it for making your favourite curry — it's your beer spoon, and that's it. And never use damaged plastic for anything sanitary, as it can harbour bacteria. And forget about wood — bacteria loves wood.

### POLYESTER HOP BAGS, ONE PER HOP ADDITION

- When hops are added to the kettle, these inexpensive bags are used to contain your hop pellets. They make hop separation easy when you've finished boiling in a standard pot or kettle, although they do restrict the hop extraction you can achieve because the hops aren't loosely moving around in the kettle.
- Keep a few on hand, including extras. Trying to take a boiling-hot hop bag out of your kettle to add more hops to it isn't much fun. They're relatively inexpensive, and it's better to have too many than too few.
- These bags are reusable. Rinse them off, let them dry, then pack them away with your kit. They don't need to be washed with detergent or sanitised, as they're added to the boil and disinfected from the heat of the boil. They will take on the colour of wort, and that's okay — just be sure you get all the vegetable and protein off them, and that they are thoroughly dried before stashing them away.

## CAN OPENER OR SCISSORS

- Malt extract in syrup form is sold in tins; in powdered form it is packed in plastic bags — so you just need the right tool to open the tin or bag.

## KITCHEN SCALES

- You'll need these for weighing your hops and malt extract. A set that registers up to 1 kg (2 lb 4 oz) is sufficient, provided it measures to the gram. It's the lower side that's more important — you can always weigh malt extract in batches to get to the quantity you need, whereas some recipes only need a few grams of hops, so that specificity is more important.

## FERMENTER

- A 25 litre (6½ gallon) food-grade plastic bucket with lid and tap.
- Your batch size will be 19 litres (5 gallons), but that's our target volume for bottling. There is waste along the way, so we need a fermenter that can hold more than 19 litres. Ferments also expand as the yeast grows and the characteristic foam ('krausen') forms. The rule of thumb is to use a vessel 25% larger than your target volume, or roughly 25 litres (6½ gallons) in our case.
- The lid must seal well, and needs to do so over and over again. For the sake of the planet, and your wallet, avoid single-use buckets.

## AIRLOCK AND STOPPER

- Along with a tight-sealing lid, an airlock and stopper create a one-way valve, allowing the carbon dioxide produced during fermentation to vent off, without allowing in any air — which is full of bacteria. The airlock is inserted into the stopper, and the stopper into the lid of your fermenter. Airlocks come in a few forms that vary in terms of cost and ease of cleaning.
- One type of airlock is the **bubbler** — an inexpensive piece of clear plastic with an S-shaped pathway through it, much like the S-bend in the plumbing under your sink that traps sewer gas from leaking up. Unfortunately, bubblers are very difficult to clean, so I say avoid them. The initial cost savings will be outweighed by the fact that you constantly have to throw them away when you can't clean out the mould-forming krausen that inevitably gets lodged in them.

Fermenter bucket,
assembled with a
'three-piece' airlock
and tap, to create a
sealed environment where
gas can escape, but air
cannot enter

- My personal go-to is a **three-piece option**. They're usually made from thicker plastic than the bubblers, which makes them more durable. They can also be opened, and all the internal workings can be accessed with a sponge for cleaning.
- As you graduate into other vessels like purpose-built fermenters, a simple hose into a bucket of water is another option. This method consists of a hose running out of the very top of your fermentation vessel, where gas can vent, into a bucket of water, with the other end of the hose fixed below the surface of the water. As the pressure builds inside the fermenter, the gas will bubble out of the fermenter, travelling up through the hose and down into the bucket of water. The hose effectively acts as a one-way valve, allowing gas to vent out of the fermenter, but stopping air and bacteria getting through the water and up into the hose. How far below the surface of the water the hose is submerged will determine how much pressure needs to build before a bubble will exit the hose. In a purpose-built home-brew fermenter, one of the in-built features will be a fitting, at the highest point on top of the fermenter, for a hose to be attached.

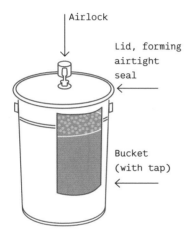

Airlock

Lid, forming
airtight
seal

Bucket
(with tap)

Simple 'hose and bucket' fermenter

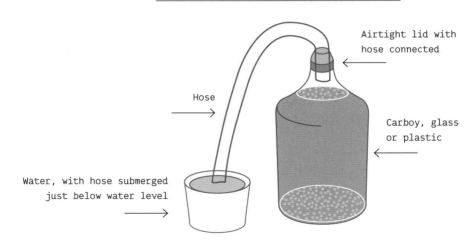

Airtight lid with
hose connected

Hose

Carboy, glass
or plastic

Water, with hose submerged
just below water level

## Make your own fermenter bucket

If you don't feel like paying for the convenience of a bucket with a tap installed, you can drill your own holes with a correctly sized drill bit. Most taps and stoppers sold at home-brew shops take a 1 cm (½ inch) bit, but check your tap and rubber stopper. Here's how it's done.

1. Drill the hole on the lid somewhere near the middle. This is for the airlock and stopper, and placement isn't critical.

2. Positioning the hole on the side of the bucket, where the tap will go, is important. Too low and you'll struggle to make a seal, and will pull through too much yeast after the ferment. Too high and you'll leave behind valuable beer! Place the hole at a height from the bottom where the tap's lowest point, when inserted, will sit just below the bottom of the bucket. This may seem odd, but is the right height for the amount of yeast you'll have. And the tap can be turned while in use, to allow the bucket to sit flat.

3. Clean up the plastic burrs. Any plastic left over after drilling will affect your seal when installing your tap and airlock.

4. Check for leaks!

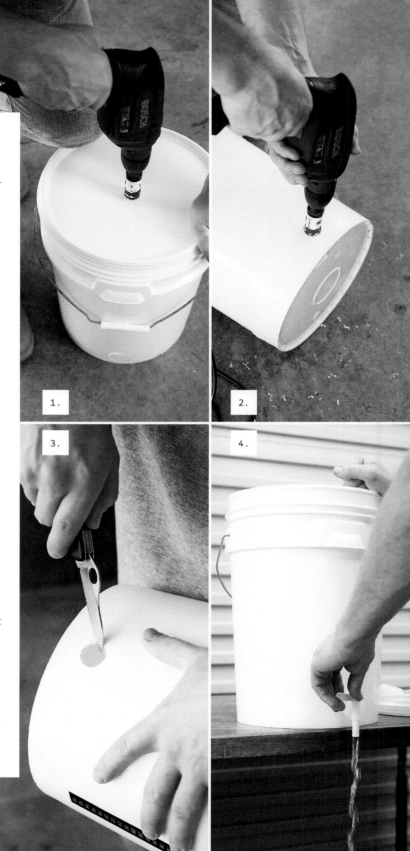

1.

2.

3.

4.

### THERMOMETER

- So much of brewing is temperature dependent — when to pitch your yeast, and what temperature your fermenting beer is at, are vital pieces of information. There are two types of thermometers, both helpful in different types of brewing.
- **Stick-on thermometer strips** are very cost effective, and fairly accurate, and you stick them onto the outside of your plastic fermenter. They give you a reading on the temperature within the fermenter, without you having to open the lid to put a glass thermometer in your beer — two good ways to contaminate your beer if you're not careful.
- A **glass thermometer** is more accurate than the stick-on, but must be properly sanitised and handled carefully. It's also essential when you graduate to working with specialty grains. It won't be used in the boil, so the glass shouldn't shatter and ruin your batch of beer. Metal versions are fine as well, provided the probe can be sanitised.

### 500 ML (2 CUP) PLASTIC, GLASS OR METAL MEASURING CUP

- This must be heat tolerant; a lid would be a bonus. It will be used to hydrate yeast, and therefore must be a container you can sanitise. The same rules regarding plastic apply — if it gets a scratch inside, get a new one.
- The lid is there to keep bacteria from drifting into your measuring cup. If your container doesn't have a lid, aluminium foil will do.

### ICE CUBES

- This is to create a water bath in which you'll cool your wort. You'll need one or two bags from your local convenience store. More is better, but it's up to you how much you want to spend on it.

### HYDROMETER (OPTIONAL)

- A hydrometer is a device that measures the density, or 'gravity', of a liquid. In our case, it measures the concentration of sugar in our wort. By measuring the gravity of the wort before and after fermentation, we can determine how much sugar has been consumed and converted into alcohol. This essentially tells you when the yeast is done. More specifically, it tells you your beer's starting and finishing gravities, from which you will determine the attenuation level, residual sugar, and percentage of alcohol by volume (ABV) resulting from your ferment.

# Method #2:
# Extract brewing plus specialty grains

Specialty grains are a pretty simple addition to extract brewing, but with an outsized positive impact on the final result of the beer. The additional tools cost a nominal amount, the additional time is insignificant — and the added complexity is no more than making a cup of tea. The benefits include fuller and richer beer, and access to nearly every style imaginable. A pretty good deal.

Malt extract is still used as the base, or the source of most of the fermentable sugars. The beer is then customised using specialty grains. Colour, flavour and mouthfeel are all impacted by whatever combination of grains you choose. Time to get creative!

To get started, the kettle is filled with water and heated to roughly 65°C (149°F). The cracked specialty grains are added to a large polyester bag, making a big teabag. The teabag is added to the kettle and allowed to steep for 30 minutes. It's then removed, placed in a strainer, over the kettle. Additional water at no more than 78°C (172°F) is then poured over the grains, to rinse any remaining sugar and flavour from the grains into the kettle. From there, the kettle is heated back to a boil, and the process is the same as the extract-brewing method above.

**ADDITIONAL TOOLS FOR EXTRACT BREWING**
**WITH SPECIALTY GRAINS**

- A **malt mill** — or you can have your grains milled by a home-brew shop.
- A **grain bag**, made from woven polyester, or another similar material that is heat resistant and flavour neutral.
- A **thermometer** for monitoring the grain steeping temperature.
- A **pasta strainer**, or similar, to hold the grain-filled bag over your kettle while the grains are being rinsed.

**Specialty grains equipment**

1. Malt mill
2. Grain bag
3. Thermometer
4. Pasta strainer

# Malt mills and grain freshness

While dried malt does have a pretty long shelf life of 1–2 years, it's still best used fresh — and its freshness goes downhill very quickly once the grain has been cracked, which happens during milling. By cracking the grain you're breaking its husk (its outer layer of protection), and exposing the kernel to the moisture in the air, accelerating the staling process.

If you get to the point where you buy a few kilos of malt that you use often and will last you for a few brews, you'll want to buy your own mill and crack your grains on brew day. You can skip this investment, and let your home-brew shop mill your malt for you — as long as you use the cracked grains straight away.

When you get to all-grain brewing, I strongly encourage you to buy a malt mill. This will give you control over how fine your crush is, to better dial in your process to suit your equipment, as you can't trust the home-brew shop to always do this for you. Also, different grains, like barley versus wheat, will also require a different crush. And even different barley varieties will grow to different sizes and require a different crush. These are all variables you will want to control yourself.

Malt mills are available in a few different shapes, but they all work in the same way. Grain is added to a hopper, which feeds the grain into a roller. When the roller is turned, the grain is pressed between the roller and the side of the mill housing and cracked open. The gap between the roller and the mill housing can be narrowed or widened to achieve the best crush for the grain kernel size you're brewing with.

# Method #3: All-grain brewing

With all-grain brewing, you're getting your fermentable sugar from grain only; no malt extract is used. It's making beer from scratch — totally customisable, with unlimited creative potential.

The upside is endless. The downside is you need a lot more equipment. All-grain is a huge world of brewing that changes faster than this book can be published, so I'll focus on the top-level concept.

### TOP-NOTCH GEAR FOR ALL-GRAIN BREWING

Not much of your extract brewing kit is still relevant. Since you're creating your own fermentable sugar, you need a mash tun. Reasonably priced kits are available to turn a picnic cooler into a perfectly effective mash tun. You also need a kettle large enough to boil the full volume of your wort. And since you can't safely lift the kettle when it's full of wort, you need to modify the kettle with an outlet to get the liquid out — which requires some moderately complex stainless steel and plumbing work.

A full wort boil is also tough to achieve on most domestic stoves, so you will likely also need to move into a new space outside, or if you're lucky enough into a dedicated brewery space with a high BTU burner or properly sized electric element (and proper ventilation and safety equipment). And since you can't lift the kettle full of wort, you can't place it in the sink to cool — and you probably don't have a sink big enough anyway. So you will need to build or buy a wort chiller. It's all very manageable for an avid DIY type, or can be bought if you have more money than time.

And with all this additional investment in equipment, you may want to get more beer out of it. After all, the time it takes to make 19 litres (5 gallons) is the same as making 38 litres (10 gallons) — so now you need another fermenter, or more likely, a larger purpose-built fermenter with a few features that enable more efficient and controlled ferments. Before you know it, you'll be planning home renovations to keep pace with your expanding brewery space!

If you're not the DIY type, there are also some pretty effective all-grain brewing systems loaded with features available for sale. But given the rate of innovation in the home-brewing world, I won't bother spending any time on the specifics of each, because by the time you get to this stage of your home-brewing career, there will probably be more! These systems are great in number, and manufacturers will have their own instructions on how best to use their equipment.

# Packaging your beautiful brew

Packaging is probably every brewer's least favourite part of making home brew, and refers to the process of putting beer into the vessel in which it's delivered to the drinker's mouth. As a home brewer, you'll be using bottles or kegs.

There are a handful of tools needed to put beer in bottles and kegs, and these depend on how you intend to 'condition' your beer — conditioning is the process by which you add beer's signature bubbles.

Bottles are the best place to start. They are cheaper to purchase than a keg, cheaper to manage from an ongoing cost perspective, and easier to handle. Kegs are essentially one huge bottle, so packaging day is MUCH faster, but kegs are not conducive to sharing, since all your beer is in one vessel — you can pour a beer for your friends to drink at your place, but you can't give them a bottle or two to take home. Kegs also require equipment to cool, carbonate and serve the beer. These are all manageable, but expensive and not something to rush into.

## Conditioning your beer

The two methods of adding bubbles to your beer are through 'bottle conditioning' or 'forced carbonation'.

**Bottle conditioning** means the bubbles are formed by feeding the residual yeast in your beer a small amount of sugar, just prior to putting the beer in the bottle and sealing it. The beer is held at fermentation temperature while the yeast consumes the sugar and creates carbon dioxide ($CO_2$). Unlike your main ferment, where the $CO_2$ vents off into the atmosphere, the $CO_2$ is trapped in the sealed bottle, building up the pressure. As the pressure builds in the vessel, the $CO_2$ is forced to dissolve into the beer, carbonating the liquid. It's a natural process, and has been used since the beginning of beer. The small amount of sugar used has a negligible impact on the beer's flavour and alcohol level. Once it has completed its ferment, the yeast settles to the bottom of the bottle. This flocculation process is accelerated when the bottle is chilled, and when poured by a conscientious drinker, the flocculated yeast remains in the bottle and doesn't impact their drinking experience. The whole bottle-conditioning process takes an additional 10–14 days after fermentation.

**Forced carbonation** is a more modern method of conditioning. In this version, $CO_2$ from a gas cylinder is injected into the beer through a tool that creates micro bubbles (which dissolve quickly, reappearing only when the beer is poured), or $CO_2$ is added to the top of a pressure-sealed vessel, where it dissolves into the beer over time. In the home-brew setting, force-carbonating requires a keg. For transporting small amounts of your beer, your carbonated beer can then be transferred

**Bottle conditioning is where most home brewers start, and where I recommend you start. Even if you can skip straight to kegging your beer, the natural carbonation process of bottle conditioning offers an opportunity to get what I believe is a superior flavour. It also forces you to recognise beer as being a living product. While moving to kegging is easier, and when done well can offer exceptional beer, knowing both methods will make you more fully appreciate beer, in both the home-brewing and commercial beer worlds.**

to a bottle with an additional tool, called a counter-pressure filler. Filling bottles from a keg is a slow process, but it does allow your finished beer to be shared, or entered in brewing competitions, which usually require beer submissions to be in bottles. Force-carbonating can be complicated and frustrating; adding the right amount $CO_2$ pressure to achieve the desired carbonation level in the beers isn't always as straightforward in practice as the science says it should be. It can be especially frustrating when you're in a hurry to share your beer at your weekend barbecue, but can be mastered with the right slow and methodical approach.

## Bottling gear

To get your beer in bottles you'll need a few more tools, but nothing that will break the bank. The fermented beer will be transferred off the yeast and residual sediment, blended with priming sugar, and gently transferred into the bottles, which are quickly capped, stored at ferment temperature and given time for the yeast to work its magic.

Here's what you'll need.

### BOTTLING BUCKET
- Another copy of your 25 litre (6½ gallon) fermenter — a food-grade plastic container with a lid, and a tap at the bottom of the vessel. This setup is interchangeable with your fermenter.

### FOOD-GRADE PLASTIC TUBE
- To 'rack', or transfer, your beer from your fermenter to the bottling bucket. The tube needs to be the right diameter to fit your fermenter's tap, and long enough to allow gravity to move the beer to the bottom of your bottling bucket when the fermenter is placed above it.

# *You don't need all those shiny gizmos...*

What was once a fledgling industry selling raw materials to at-home DIY types is now a full service industry with businesses selling products that attempt to fix every issue a home brewer will encounter — from stainless steel hop sacks to fully kitted-out systems that replicate commercial breweries. Most of these products do exactly what they say they do, I can't fault them for that. But there is always a cheaper alternative, so don't get concerned about buying anything beyond what I've listed above until you've done a few brews and have proven you really would benefit from the upgrade.

Despite what the manufacturers claim, all these gizmos won't make your beer better — only you can do that. A craftsperson never blames his tools, as the old saying goes...

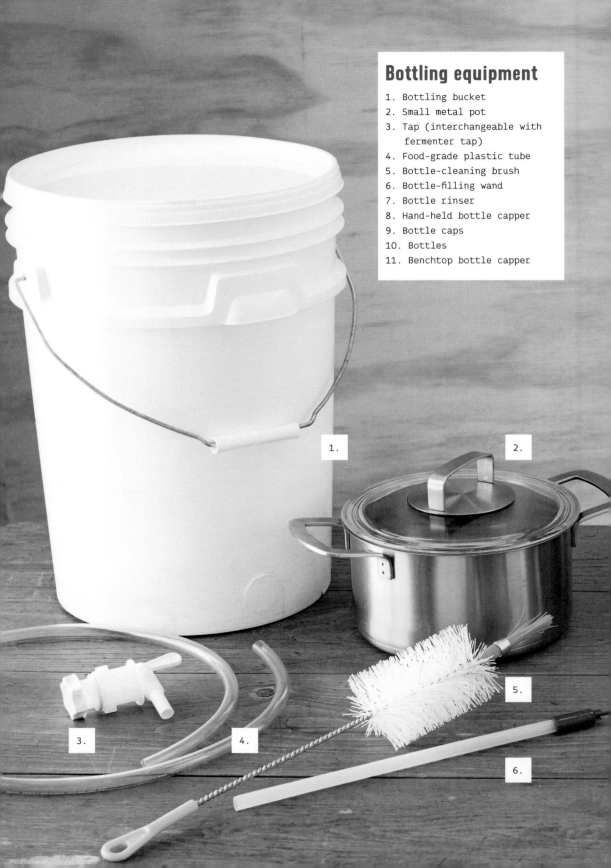

## Bottling equipment

1. Bottling bucket
2. Small metal pot
3. Tap (interchangeable with fermenter tap)
4. Food-grade plastic tube
5. Bottle-cleaning brush
6. Bottle-filling wand
7. Bottle rinser
8. Hand-held bottle capper
9. Bottle caps
10. Bottles
11. Benchtop bottle capper

1.

2.

3.

4.

5.

6.

## SMALL METAL POT

- 1 litre (35 fl oz) capacity, with a lid, to boil a small amount of water to sanitise the water and dissolve your priming sugar into. The lid will sanitise in the process of boiling the water, and will keep bacteria out as the solution cools.

## BOTTLES

- What you want are those thick brown glass 'crown seal' bottles — also called 'pry-off' bottles — of 640–750 ml (22–26 fl oz) capacity. No twist-top or twist-off bottles, and no bottles of any other colour.
- Twist-tops don't seal well, and tend to be made of thinner glass.
- All other colours will allow too much light to reach your beer, causing a signature 'skunk' aroma. (If you live in a country that doesn't have skunks, it's the smell the animal secretes to fend off predators and save its life. It's not pleasant, and you don't want it in your beer.) No fancy-coloured glass is worth making crap beer.
- The larger 750 ml or 640 ml bottles are handy because they mean you only have to clean, sanitise and fill half as many as the smaller 330–375 ml (11–13 fl oz) ones. Why process two bottles when you need only process one? But if you want to use smaller bottles, they are perfectly fine.
- For each 19 litre (5 gallon) batch of beer, you'll need about 26 x 750 ml bottles, or about 30 x 640 ml bottles. It's always good to have a few extra bottles on hand — it's so much easier than scrambling to clean and sanitise a few bottles halfway through your bottling run!

## BOTTLE RINSER

- A bottle rinser is a device that hooks up to your water source and rinses an inverted bottle. It is used when a bottle has been cleaned with detergent, which then needs to be rinsed out. You can get away with filling and emptying the bottle a few times to rinse it, but having a spray into an inverted bottle that is draining the whole time is way more efficient in both time and water. It's not essential, but is one of those tools I actually recommend buying.

## BOTTLING WAND

- This is a simple valve mechanism made of plastic that fits to the end of your plastic tube and can be inserted into your bottles. The spring-loaded valve holds the beer until you press it into the bottom

**PLASTIC — NOT FANTASTIC!**
It's best to avoid plastic PET bottles. I have yet to see a PET bottle that can match the light-blocking attributes of brown glass. They're really hard to clean and can easily scratch, making them impossible to sanitise. There are no commercial brewers I know of using PET bottles — trust the experts on this one. The cheapest bottle is one you get for free when you buy a nice beer, so head to your local brewery or independent bottle shop, buy a few bombers of something that sounds interesting, and before you know it you'll have all the bottles you need!

of the bottle, breaking the seal of the valve and allowing beer to flow. When the bottle is full, you remove the pressure and the valve closes.

## BOTTLE CAPS

- Also called crown seals, bottle caps are inexpensive and sold at all home-brew shops.

## BOTTLE CAPPER

- This device crimps the ends of the bottle caps around the neck of the bottles, creating a seal.
- There are three main styles — but this is another instance where I suggest you spend some money on the more advanced, and simpler, bench capper. This type secures the bottle, to stop it tipping over during capping, and ensures a good seal.
- There is a more manual hand-held version that will give a good seal, but it's less stable and prone to tipping over.
- The third type is very inexpensive, but requires weight or a whack from a mallet to seal; whacking the top of a beer bottle to seal it seems counter-intuitive. It can be done, but it's a slow process, and subject to inconsistently sealed bottles, which will mean inconsistently carbonated beers — too much work has gone into getting your beer to this stage to waste time with a cheap capper.

# Kegging: A big step up

Switching from bottling to kegging is a momentous occasion for a home brewer. Eventually, the time committed to bottling catches up to the cost of buying the additional equipment, and the brewer bites the bullet and splurges on their very own draft system.

Kegging is essentially like filling one huge bottle instead of 30–60 smaller bottles. Kegs can be $CO_2$ purged prior to filling them with beer, prolonging your hoppy beer's vibrancy, and slowing staling, so all your beers taste fresher for longer.

But without removing the shelves from your kitchen fridge, you can't fit a keg in it — so you'll need a second fridge to keep your keg cold in. You'll also need an expensive $CO_2$ regulator and a gas bottle, a keg, and some dispensing fittings. The costs are significant — but if you value the freshest possible beer, are exhausted by bottling, or just love the idea of tap beer at home, go for it!

*Chapter Five*

# SANITATION

Now that you have your brewing and bottling equipment, and know what each piece is for, it's time to learn how to clean it, sanitise it and store it. That may sound very straightforward, and for the most part it is — but this is not an area you can skimp on if you want to be a good brewer. Every brewer I respect, and whose beer I enjoy, knows the importance of cleaning and proper sanitation.

## That's clean enough...right? Wrong.

Let's get down to some basics. Cleaning is the practice of removing visible organic matter and debris from a benchtop or piece of equipment.

Something is 'clean' when it has been wiped down with a cloth or sponge — which may or may not have a detergent on it that's designed to break down organic matter or oils — and is then rinsed with hot water and allowed to dry.

'Clean' is sufficient for your kitchen at home, and for anything used in brewing that's on the 'hot side' — those things that come in contact with the wort while it's at or near a boil (100°C/212°F), like your kettle and brewing spoon.

But in the brewery, 'clean' is just step one. Something that is 'clean' is still teeming with microscopic life — including the dreaded beer-spoiling bacteria. These bacteria are harmless to your food, and for the most part to you, but they will quickly multiply in a batch of fresh wort much faster than your yeast can, and they will ruin it. That's why brewers don't stop at 'clean'.

## SANITISED is clean enough!

In brewing, we want all our equipment that comes in contact with fresh wort to be cleaned, and then sanitised.

Sanitation can be achieved with minimal cost and with relatively safe chemicals, but it doesn't kill 100% of the beer-spoiling bacteria. That's okay — we know we will never kill all the little critters, but if we reduce their numbers enough, they won't be able to reproduce fast enough to colonise our wort before our yeast does.

Bacteria and yeast are two opposing forces, both designed to grow until there is no more food to consume. Whichever has the bigger population in our ferment when the food — in our case the wort — is added will outgrow the other. We sanitise our equipment to reduce the bacteria population, and then pitch a large quantity of yeast cells that will be well positioned to outgrow the bacteria.

**All your equipment that comes in contact with your wort once it's been chilled — called the 'cold side' — needs to be sanitised.**

Fermenters, airlocks and stoppers, and all the bottling equipment need to be sanitised. Your yeast-handling equipment, and anything being added to the fermenter (such as a thermometer or a hop sack), also needs to be sanitised.

One rule of thumb in sanitising is that if you can see debris, you do not have a sanitary environment — go back and clean it again before you try to sanitise it.

Stainless steel brewing equipment is superior to plastic because it's sturdy and is tougher to scratch. But stainless costs a small fortune, so it's perfectly fine to stick with plastic, provided you take good care of it and replace it when it gets damaged.

Once plastic is scratched, it becomes very difficult to be certain it has been sanitised. A scratch that's so small you can barely see it is still large enough for bacteria to find a home. And because a single bacteria cell is smaller than a water molecule, bacteria cells can make themselves cozy in that scratch, out of reach of your water-based sanitiser that won't be able to squeeze into the scratch and neutralise the bacteria. And those little bacteria cells are hungry and horny and can't wait to multiply in your wort and excrete all kinds of funky flavours.

So protect your plastic fermenters. Use them for beer only — no fishing tackle or makeshift sandcastle moulds please. Store them with the lid on to keep out dust, and always put them away clean and dry.

## Sterilised: why not kill them all?

There is a step up from sanitised, and that's sterilised. Sterile is free from 100% of bacteria.

Sterilisation is important in laboratories and hospitals with higher stakes than a brewery. Nature wants us to have beer — that's evident time and time again with the small miracles that make the brewing process possible. One such miracle is the ability of yeast to crowd out trace levels of bacteria, keeping their flavour-spoiling impact to below human taste thresholds, so sterilisation is not needed in the brewery. Sanitation is sufficient.

If you can see debris, you do not have a sanitary environment.

Iodophor

Water for making a
sanitiser solution

# Know your weapons: sanitisers and detergents

As we said above, 'clean' is not the same as 'sanitised'. To clean a piece of equipment in your home brewery you need a sponge, some elbow grease and a home-brew detergent.

## HOME-BREW DETERGENTS

Home-brew detergents are specifically formulated with agents that are selected because they do a good job neutralising the materials left over in the beer making process — specifically the organic matter in the 'krausen' of a fermentation.

Krausen is the foam formed in the ferment, and when it subsides as the yeast finishes, it leaves a line of debris at the top of your fermenter that marks the high watermark of the foam in the ferment. This foam line consists of dried-on yeast, proteins, trub and hop particles. As it dries, it becomes very sticky, and is best removed with a detergent that attacks its individual components. Your typical domestic dish soap will work in a pinch, but it's designed to clean greasy pots and pans. It may also have a lemon scent that can penetrate your plastic and leach out into your next batch of beer.

If you run out of home-brew detergent and use domestic soap, be sure to thoroughly rinse your equipment with extremely hot water.

## SANITISERS

Sanitation is the next step following a thorough wash and rinse of your equipment. To sanitise your equipment you need cool water and a home-brewing sanitiser.

The most basic, and in my unscientific opinion, most effective home-brewing sanitiser is **iodophor** — an iodine based sanitiser that is safe, effective and very economical. There are a number of sanitisers on the market that have been designed to improve on the effectiveness of

## *Super important takeaway tips*

- - - - - - - - - - - - - - - - - - - - - - - - - - - - - - - - - - - - - - - - - - - - - - - - - - - - - - - - - - - - - - - - - - - - - - -

- **'Clean' is not 'sanitary' — you must perform the two actions separately.**
- **If you see dirt on your equipment, you can't sanitise it.**
- **During brew day, store some of the sanitiser you used on your fermenter in a bowl or a spray bottle, so you can wipe down your workspace and sanitise things on the go. It may not give you 100% sanitation, but it's better than nothing.**
- **Beware of tools and chemicals being marketed that claim to make your life easier. Most have unintended consequences — and there's no replacement for diligence, planning and hard work in a brewery.**

iodophor and solve 'problems' for home brewers, but I have never come across one that does everything it says without some more significant, unintended consequences.

One such 'problem' with using iodophor is that it stains equipment, leaving a yellow tint on vinyl hoses and plastic fermenters. But this staining is just cosmetic: it will not leach into your beer and change its colour, nor will it change its flavour. Another drawback is the 20 minutes iodophor takes to work, but I find a little thought given to your brew day is enough to ensure there is no wasted time. I have solely used iodophor in all my home brewing and have never had a spoiled batch, or one with chemical taint. So my advice is to use iodophor until you discover a problem one of the other sanitisers promises to solve. And if you can't source iodophor, give whatever your local home-brew shop suggests a try.

Sanitisers need contact time to be effective. In the case of iodophor, you will make a solution in your fermenter that fills the entire surface of the fermenter, then place all your equipment in that solution to soak for 20 minutes. Other acid-based sanitisers require much less solution, as they foam and coat the surface of your equipment; the foaming maintains contact for the 1–2 minutes required to effectively sanitise your equipment. With these sanitisers, a litre of solution can be mixed in your fermenter and shaken to coat the interior, or in a spray bottle and sprayed onto the surfaces to be sanitised. I prefer soaking because it ensures no surfaces are missed, particularly in hard-to-reach places like interior surfaces of airlocks, hosing and bottles.

### Before buying a sanitiser, make sure of two things

First, it has to be a no-rinse formula. Believe it or not, the tap water that you would use to rinse your equipment may contain enough bacteria to undo the sanitation efforts of the solution you're rinsing away. Use a no-rinse formula and allow it to drip dry.

Second, be cautious of anything that claims to do everything. A detergent that also sanitises is one such example. Detergents are designed to do things that are different to sanitisers. I'm not a scientist, but I don't understand how both actions can be achieved from the same chemical without compromising both its cleaning and sanitising actions. Do your research.

### Read the directions and stay safe

Whatever product you use, be mindful of the directions and any risks. Some products are sold in dangerous concentrations, and all should be treated with care. All home-brewing chemicals are relatively safe, as there are set standards for the safety of hobbyists — but that's no reason to let your guard down. Keep them away from pets and small children, and store in a cool place in the house.

# LET'S BREW!

Chapter Six

The beer brewing process is series of physical manipulations to encourage a natural reaction to occur. As brewers, we use our brewing equipment to set the stage, and nature does the heavy lifting. The more we control nature, the more consistent the outcome.

As home brewers we can make some pretty tasty beer using basic equipment, and easy to handle raw materials. At the entry level of the spectrum, where we use only malt extract, it's difficult to achieve exactly the beer we want to target — but that's totally fine. While you can't make a perfect clone of your favourite commercial beer, we can still have a lot of fun, make some very satisfying beers, and learn a lot about the process of fermentation and the impacts of the various specialty malts, hops and yeast strains — all very important skills needed to progress to the next level.

As your desire to hit a target style of beer increases, and you can allocate some time and money to building up your brewery, you can add a few bits of process-control equipment and start to really dial in your recipes and ferments.

Eventually, many home brewers want to break through the limitations of malt extract, and further customise their beers by starting from grain and running a mash themselves. This step to all-grain brewing, as discussed in the Equipment chapter on page 109, requires space and a significant amount of gear (which means outlaying money!), but enables you to make nearly any beer imaginable.

In this section I'll lay out, step by step, the process for making your first malt-extract beer through to the start of fermentation.

In the following sections, I'll explain in more detail how to ferment your wort, then get your beer into bottles or kegs and carbonate it. We'll then look at the additional steps needed to customise your beer through the use of specialty malts. We'll also take a step sideways to discuss liquid yeast and how to prepare a yeast starter.

Let's get brewing.

## Time for some serious fun!

One of the home-brewing community's earliest writers and visionaries, Charlie Papazian, coined the phrase, 'Relax, and have a home brew'. I don't advocate drinking and brewing (at least not until the yeast is pitched), but his message is very applicable when learning to brew. It's meant to be fun! You won't make perfect beer on your first try, so relax, and just make some beer. I expect that on some level, it will be the most satisfying beer you ever drink.

## Just one last thing...

Before we get started, there is one last small but essential piece of equipment you must get yourself: **a notebook**.

Every recipe you make should be recorded. If you experiment with a new malt and love the result, but didn't record the amount you used, you won't be able to repeat that success.

Information on the time it took you to complete each step can be helpful when planning future brew days — knowing how long a pot of water takes to boil on your stove means you can figure out how much of the sanitising process you need to do before putting your water on to boil. Knowing how long the cooling process takes helps determine when to start your yeast. And most importantly, recording the temperature and activity of your ferment, as well as the time since you pitched your yeast, will enable you to make improvements on your next batch.

To sum all that up: **record what you do**, so you can improve next time.

## Your first malt extract batch

For your first batch we'll keep things simple. We'll target a beer with 5% alcohol, and 25 IBUs.*

The exact type of malt extract and hops variety you use doesn't matter much — the point of this first batch is to learn to ferment, even if you make a few mistakes.

However the two beers I suggest you choose from are a:

- **Pale Ale** using light malt extract + American Cascade hops + a neutral American Ale yeast
- **Brown Ale** using dark malt extract + English Fuggles hops + an estery English Ale yeast.

\* IBUs, or International Bittering Units, are a rating of the quantity of bitter-tasting compounds dissolved in the wort. The scale starts at zero and in theory has no ceiling, but in practice ends around 100. In general, a low IBU rating of 5–10 says a beer will not taste very bitter at all, and a beer with around 80 IBUs has the potential to be quite bitter. But as you travel up the IBU scale, you will often find brewers using malt and residual sweetness to balance the bitterness — so the flavour, and perceived bitterness, won't always be the same on the palate across different beers at the same IBU level.

## Now plan ahead

A big part of brewing is planning. **The weekend before** you plan to brew, head to the home-brew store and get everything you need. Put the hops in the freezer, and the yeast and malt extract in the fridge.

**The day before** you brew, buy a couple of bags of ice and, if you plan to use it, some spring water. (Or if your tap water is very minerally, boil it up and let it cool overnight — see Magic trick #3.)

The best way to mess up a batch of beer is by running to the store mid brew for an essential item, so plan ahead.

As well as the equipment in chapter 4, here's what you'll need.

- Malt extract: 3 kg (6¾ lb) light malt extract **OR** dark malt extract, dry or liquid
- Hops: 45 g (1½ oz) US Cascade hops (7% AA), **OR** 70 g (2½ oz) UK Fuggle hops (4.5% AA); AA refers to the alpha acid composition of the hops
- Hop sack: one sack will do, since we have only one hop addition
- Yeast: one 11 g (¼ oz) packet of American Ale **OR** English Ale yeast
- Home-brew detergent
- Home-brew sanitiser
- Kettle finings
- Yeast nutrient
- Priming sugar*
- Bottle caps
- Ice: two or three bags
- Water (if not using tap water): 12–15 litres (3–4 gallons) of bottled water to top up your fermenter.

* **Priming sugar is a small quantity of dextrose that will give yeast in the bottles a little something to feed on, to produce enough $CO_2$ to carbonate the beer.**

# Magic trick #3: Purifying tap water

If your tap water is very 'heavy', you can boil off the chemicals and minerals the day before brewing with it. Ideally, you should boil up 25 litres (6½ gallons) — your batch size, allowing for some evaporation. However, you'll need a very big pot and maybe even a stronger heat source if your kitchen stove isn't heavy-duty enough to boil so much liquid. As the water cools overnight, with the lid on the pot at all times, the minerals should form a white chalky substance on the bottom of the pot. When it comes to brew time, you can then carefully pour off the water, leaving the minerals behind.

This isn't a required process, and not a complication I suggest tackling on your first brew. If after a few beers you can still taste something you don't like that carries through from your tap water, consider giving this a try. In the meantime, just know it's an option.

# Making the wort

→ Fill your kettle with tap water to two-thirds or three-quarters of its capacity. Too high and we might cause a boil-over; too low and you'll need to add more chlorinated tap water to the fermenter — it's better to have more wort in your pot for the hops to move around in. Make a note of the approximate distance from the top of the kettle to the top of the water level. A rough estimate in inches or millimetres is fine.

→ Set the burner on high and bring your water to a boil. If you have a smaller sized electric stove, you may need to put your kettle across two burners to get up to a boil in a reasonable time. If you have a lid, this is one those times when it's okay to use it.

- Remember to jot down the start time on the burner and when you get to the boil. This way you'll know for next time how much time you have to prepare other things.

While we're waiting for the water to boil, let's get your fermenter sanitised. The following assumes you're using iodophor or a similar sanitiser that requires a 20-minute soak to be effective.

→ Make sure the tap on your fermenter is properly fitted and closed.

→ Begin filling the fermenter with cool water.

- Hot water will volatise off the bacteria-killing agents in most sanitisers. For this reason, only use cool tap water when mixing your sanitiser.

→ Place your lid, airlock, stopper and a small spoon in the bottom of the fermenter. Since the lid is larger than the opening of the bucket, turn the lid on its side and push it into the bucket. The mouth of the bucket will have to bend to accept the lid, which is fine; it's plastic, so it can handle it. Make sure the entire lid is below the mouth of the bucket, so it can be fully submerged in the sanitiser.

→ Check the tap for leaks. There may be plastic burrs that stop the tap gaskets sitting flush and creating a seal. It's much better to find and fix a leak now, than when you have your finished wort in the fermenter!

→ While the water is still being added, add the recommended dose of sanitiser to the filling water, so it gets well mixed in.

→ Make sure your airlock is completely full of sanitiser. If it's upside down and has an air bubble trapped in it, that part where the air bubble is sitting is not in contact with sanitiser, and therefore won't be sanitised!

→ As the water level reaches the top, open the tap to allow some sanitiser to fill the tap and come in contact with the inner surfaces. Do this over a drain, or a small vessel, to catch the sanitiser so you don't have to waste time cleaning your floor.

→ Let everything soak for at least 20 minutes. Longer isn't an issue.

**Check on the kettle to see if it's boiling. If it's boiling like crazy, check to see how much water, if any, has evaporated, using the approximate level you recorded earlier. If you've boiled off a lot — perhaps the sanitation took a while — add a bit more water and return it to a boil.**

→ When your water has reached a boil, turn off the heat.

→ Carefully remove about 100 ml (3½ fl oz) of boiling water and put it in your small measuring cup. This water, when cooled, will be used to rehydrate your yeast. The boiling water will sanitise the measuring cup, but it will need to be covered with a lid or some aluminium foil to ensure no bacteria finds its way in as the water cools below pasteurisation temperature.

→ Open your bags of dry malt extract and gently pour them into the water in your kettle. If it seems like a lot and that it won't all fit, give it a little stir using your long-handled spoon and add some more — you'll be surprised how much malt extract will dissolve in your water! Dried malt extract is very light and will go up in a cloud with the slightest

encouragement, so handle it carefully to avoid making a mess. It also becomes very sticky when steam hits it — this might impact your ability to pour it, so make sure you cut a good-sized hole in the bag.

- Pour the malt extract in gently, because it will react with the heat of the water and turbulence of the boil. If it's added too fast, it can foam over the top of the kettle — a mistake I made on my mother's new stove that cost me hours of cleaning, and years of embarrassing stories. Add a bit, let it settle, then add some more. Repeat this until it's all added.

- The other reason it's vital that the heat be off when adding the malt extract is that it will sink to the bottom of the kettle. If the heat is on, the malt extract can burn if it's allowed to sit there before you have time to stir it in. Burnt malt extract will leave an unpleasant, scorched flavour in your beer!
- If you're using an electric element, there will be residual heat in the coils, which has the same effect as leaving the burner on. Carefully move your pot of boiling water off the burner before adding your malt extract.

→ Stir the pot in a circular motion to create a gentle current to fully dissolve the malt extract into the water. Use your spoon to scrape the bottom of the pot, to ensure no malt extract has sunk and is coating the bottom.

→ Once you're satisfied that the malt extract is fully dissolved, turn the flame back on to medium, if using a kettle, or if using an electric stove, return the pot to the hot element and set it to medium.

**Carefully, so you don't burn your face or hands, waft that beautiful-smelling steam toward your nose and breathe it in... pause and take a moment, because life doesn't get much better than this.**

Return the wort — you now have wort! — to a boil slowly. I need to stress 'slowly' here, because you're approaching the stage where you can have a boil-over. Most of the home-brewing hobby is fun and relaxing, but with 10–12 litres (2½–3 gallons) of volatile, boiling-hot wort on your stove, this is one stage requiring 100% of your attention.

**Don't walk away from your kettle at this point. And DO NOT put the lid on to help it boil faster — this is one of the processes you want to happen slowly.**

- The protein in the wort will create foam as the wort gets closer to the boil. The foam starts to form in small amounts, but will grow to cover the entire surface of the wort. Use your spoon to break this foam up so it doesn't cover the whole surface — you want to keep an exit point for the steam.
- The foam traps steam inside the kettle, and as the boil intensifies and more steam is created and trapped, more foam will be created. This process accelerates when the entire surface of the kettle is covered, so it can easily catch you off guard and climb right out of the kettle, and you will have hot, dangerous, sticky wort all over your stovetop.
- Not only is this a waste of potential beer, it's going to be a huge waste of your time cleaning it all up. So heat your kettle slowly at this point, and use your spoon to break open a place on the surface of the wort for the steam to escape.

Pause and take a moment, because life doesn't get much better than this.

- If the foam is forming faster than you can knock it back, turn down the flame.
- If the foam is climbing right to the top, turn off the flame, and restart it when the foam calms down. (Sorry electric stove users, you can't turn off your heat — so go slow and be careful.)
- On the flip side, you might find the foam is forming too slowly, because you're being overly cautious and it is taking ages to reach a boil.
- Experience is the only way to know how high to keep your burner. Take notes so you can improve next time.
- Ingredients like hops, sugar and spices can all encourage some foam, so always be mindful of a boil-over when adding ingredients to the kettle.

**After a moment or two of a full boil, the heat of the boil will 'denature' enough protein that the foam will drop down. At this point, you have achieved your 'hot break', and your risk of a boil-over has gone down dramatically.**

→ Now that you're safely at a boil, place your hops in the sack, tie it closed so it won't open in your kettle, then place it slowly into your kettle, being mindful of foam creation.

→ Set a timer for **60 minutes** and press start.
- At **30 minutes**, you need to hydrate your kettle finings.
- At **15 minutes**, you need to add the hydrated kettle finings to the boil.

→ Take another deep breath, pat yourself on the back, and breathe in that beautiful aroma of malt and hops. You're well on your way to the most satisfying beer you've ever had.

You're well on your way to the most satisfying beer you've ever had.

**Before you walk away to post pictures on social media, let me make a few comments on the boil and its intensity, and share some commonsense safety tips.**

- First, the boil intensity: there are gentle boils and hard boils, and in brewing we're aiming for something in the middle. What does the right boil look like? We want the boil intense enough to volatise negative aromas (like chlorine), but not so intense that we evaporate too much (it's a waste of fuel). Aim for about 500 ml to 1 litre (17–35 fl oz) of evaporation.
- And regarding safety, it's never a good idea to leave a boiling pot of liquid unattended, so keep an eye on it. Keep the kids, pets and roommates away while we get to work on the fermenter and yeast, but keep checking on it and make a note about the evaporation, and adjust your heat if needed.

→ Drain the airlock and place it, the stopper and the spoon on the lid.

→ Drain the rest of the sanitiser from the fermenter. Close the tap and place the fermenter upside down on the lid, covering the other equipment. Let it sit like this to drain until it's ready to fill with your cooled wort. This will enable the excess sanitiser to drain off, and stop any bacteria floating in on stray dust.

→ Place your thermometer in the bowl of reserved sanitiser. It doesn't have to be fully submerged if it's really long, but make sure you only put the sanitised part in the wort later.

→ Go back and smell your wort. Bloody good, eh?

### Let's continue...

→ Place your fermenter over a sink or drain, with a bowl underneath. Open the tap and drain 1–2 litres (35–70 fl oz) of the sanitiser into the bowl.

→ With a clean cloth soaked in your reserved sanitiser, wipe down your benchtop.

→ Put the fermenter lid upside down on the wiped-down benchtop, so the top of the lid is touching the benchtop. The interior surface of the lid may end up coming in contact with your fermenting wort, so we don't want it to touch any surface, even one wiped down with sanitiser.

**You now have your fermenter ready, and just need to let the hops finish imparting their bitterness and all the other wonders of the boil to occur.**

→ Check the timer. At **30 minutes**, add your finings to a small bowl and cover them with water. You don't need to worry about sanitising the finings or the water, because they will be added to the boil, where they will be sterilised by the heat of the boil.

→ At **15 minutes** left on the timer, add your finings to the wort.

→ When your timer reaches **0 minutes**, turn off the kettle heat, or carefully move your pot off your electric element.

→ Being careful not to burn yourself, lift the hop bag out of the kettle using your long-handled spoon and allow it to briefly drain back into the kettle. The bag will be many times its original size, as the hops has absorbed a fair bit of wort. You want that hop-infused wort back in your kettle! Set the hop bag aside when it has finished draining.

→ Put the lid on the kettle, so no bacteria-laden dust lands in the wort. The lid will be sanitised by the steam.

**The next step is to cool the wort. To do this, we'll make an ice bath in your sink by stopping up the drain, placing the pot with the lid on it in the sink, and adding ice to the sink.**

→ Place a drain stopper or dish rag in the drain to stop the water trickling out.

→ Carefully move your kettle to the sink.

→ Add lots of ice (but not all of it) to the sink around the kettle and fill the sink with cold water, up to the level of the beer in the pot — any higher and the pot may float and could even tip over!

→ It's not necessary to drain the melted water until it's warm to the touch. At that point, remove the kettle from the sink, drain the contents and repeat the process with more ice. You may need to do this a couple of times. You're targeting a pot that is cool to the touch. If you

can hold your finger against the pot for a while with no discomfort, you're done.

**While the wort is cooling, you can rehydrate your yeast. To do this we'll pour the yeast into the cooled water in your measuring cup, and let it absorb the water it lost in the dehydration process.**

→ Take the lid, or aluminium foil, off the measuring cup, placing it on your sanitised workspace.

→ Tear or cut open your yeast packet.

→ Being careful not to touch the inside of the packet, pour the yeast into the cooled water.

→ Using the sanitised spoon from inside the fermenter, gently stir the yeast into the water and put the lid or foil back on top.

→ Place your fermenter on the floor, making sure the tap is closed!

→ Remove the kettle lid. Slowly decant the wort off the sediments ('trub') and into the fermenter, being careful to agitate the wort in the fermenter as much as possible. This process of splashing and agitating the wort into the bottom of the fermenter will encourage the maximum level of oxygen absorption. And remember, your yeast needs oxygen to grow, crowd out the bacteria, and have a healthy and complete ferment. Leave as much of the trub behind as you can; don't be greedy.

- An advanced practice is to create a whirlpool using a sanitised spoon, then to siphon the beer off the trub using a sanitised piece of vinyl tubing and siphon starter. This introduces potential bacterial contamination, but has the benefit of leaving more trub behind — however, trub in your fermenter can lead to 'off' flavours in your beer. This is a tricky process requiring some coordination and care, the combination of which outweigh the potential negative flavour issues in your first few batches. I recommend looking into this process when you are further along in your brewing journey.

**Next we need to add the wort, when sufficiently cooled, to the sanitised fermenter, top it up with water, pitch the yeast and secure the lid and airlock. Then nature does its thing.**

→ When the pot is cool to the touch, lift the kettle out of the sink and put it on the bench.

→ We want the temperature of the wort, once diluted with your water, to be roughly 19°C (66°F). If after the ice bath the wort is a bit warmer than that, the water used to dilute it should cool the wort a little further. If you're in a hot climate, you may have to cool it longer in the ice bath, or dilute it with spring water that's been in the fridge.

**Keep the kids and the dog out of the room, and close any doors or windows you can, to limit the possibility of airborne bacteria finding its way into your exposed fermenter and wort.**

→ Rest the lid on the fermenter to limit dust settling in.

→ Using the stick-on thermometer, or your sanitised glass thermometer, get a temperature reading of your wort and record it. This will help you determine if you've sufficiently cooled your wort, and will enable you to do better next time — perhaps you need a little more time in the ice bath.

→ Remove the fermenter lid and pour your bottled water, or pre-boiled and cooled tap water, aggressively into the wort. We're looking to further dissolve more oxygen.

→ Rest the lid on the fermenter again and get another temperature reading — at this stage we want the lid on as often as possible. Your wort is like a patient with no immune system, so protect it.

→ Your wort is now ideally in the 17–22°C (63–72°F) temperature range. Much cooler and your yeast will be slow to start growing, giving bacteria a head start. Much warmer and your yeast will start too quickly, and develop some 'off' flavours in your beer.

**If your wort is above 25°C (77°F), and the ambient temperature is cooler than that, put on the lid with the airlock secured, and wait for it to cool.**

**If you're in a hot climate above 25°C (77°F), and the wort is only going to get warmer, go ahead and pitch your yeast. This is an example of the lack of control we as beginner home brewers have. It won't ruin your beer, so don't stress — you just learned something that will benefit you when making your next batch. There's still time to limit the 'off' flavours and rescue your beer — more on this and other common trouble-shooting issues later in chapter 7.**

**If your wort is colder than 17°C (63°F), proceed anyway. It will warm up with the yeast added. And try to do better next time — spend less time in the ice bath, or if you diluted with cold water from the refrigerator, use slightly warmer water next time.**

**The point is to think about what you can do next time and write it down so you can always be getting better at brewing.**

→ Remove the lid or foil from your yeast.

→ Using your sanitised spoon, stir the yeast again so the clumps all dissolve into an easy-to-pour liquid.

→ Remove the lid from your fermenter and pour in the yeast.

→ Secure the stopper to the lid, and the airlock to the stopper.

→ Fully secure the lid to the fermenter, being sure to hear it 'click' into place.

→ Fill your airlock with the correct amount of water, depending on the type you bought.

→ Very gently press down on the lid. If all is properly sealed, the water level in the airlock will move (press on the lid gently, with just enough effort to make the water level move).

→ Carefully move your fermenter to a cool, dark place that maintains a relatively constant temperature.
- A room with direct sunlight will warm up during the day, increasing the temperature of your ferment.
- A room with dramatic cooling at night might trick the yeast into stopping their ferment — yeast is sensitive to cold shocks.
- Also be mindful of overly active ferments — don't put the fermenter on carpet, in a closet with

clothes, or anywhere that's tough to clean. Spending a couple of minutes on a home-brewing blog will yield countless stories of ferments climbing through airlocks and leaking taps, and krausen-clogged airlocks causing a $CO_2$ buildup that eventually bursts a fermenter lid, spraying yeast and beer all over the place!

**Now that your yeast is pitched and your fermenter is in a safe, cool place, open your fridge, grab a beer and enjoy it while you clean up your tools and jot down your notes on how to improve the next one. Well done!**

# Fermenting + Maturing your wort

So your beer is now in your fermenter. From here, the yeast will do the work, but you still need to maintain a happy workplace for it. For yeast, the best working conditions are a constant and correct temperature with no direct sunlight. And your beer will benefit from being left undisturbed, so try to leave it somewhere out of the way.

For this reason, this section isn't so much a step by step, but a discussion of what's happening in your fermentation vessel.

## Fermentation: what you need to do

As an entry-level brewer, you have limited control over the temperature, so just do your best and don't stress. Keep your fermenter out of direct sunlight, so it doesn't absorb any additional heat. The activity of the yeast will create its own heat, so don't be surprised when the temperature of the beer rises as fermentation kicks off.

If you're in an extreme hot or cold climate, limit your brewing to those times of year when the weather is moderate, or be prepared for slower ferments (when cold), and more 'estery' beer (when hot). You may not make the best-tasting beer when brewing in extreme temperatures, but as I've said already, it will still be satisfying because of the love you put into it. And you'll begin to understand the nuances that occur when yeast is made to operate outside of its preferred conditions. Don't let any imperfect beers deter you from brewing — instead investigate tools or practices that will yield better flavour in your conditions.

You may even consider moving to yeast strains that suit the conditions you're in — English Ale strains traditionally run warmer than American Ale strains, and some witbier and saison strains benefit from an even warmer fermentation temperature. Lager yeast likes cold — use that to your advantage in winter.

Also important during a ferment is to leave the beer undisturbed. In addition to the yeast chewing through all the sugar and converting it to carbon dioxide, alcohol and flavour, there is also a process of sedimentation happening. This is where hop matter, grain particles and trub all drop by gravity to the bottom of the fermenter. This process is natural and results in clearer beer — so don't touch your fermenter, and let it run its course. These materials can easily be stirred up into the beer if it's bumped or agitated, so when the time comes to move your fermenter to empty it, do so carefully, slowly and gently.

Keep your notebook near your fermenter and check on it frequently. Record:

- the **time** — both the time of day, but also the number of hours since pitching your yeast
- the **activity** of the airlock — how often is it bubbling? Every second? Every 10 seconds?
- the **temperature** of the fermenter — this is when the stick-on thermometer is very handy; having to sanitise a glass thermometer, and open your fermenter to put it inside, exposes your beer to bacterial infection and the staling effects of oxygen.

All this data won't be immediately useful, but as you collect data on a number of ferments, you'll start to see a pattern, and you'll be able to adjust how long you give your beer to finish fermenting, and how much effort you want to give in maintaining a particular temperature.

If you love the taste of your beer, you'll want to try your best to re-create the same temperature during your next ferment — and if you didn't write it down, you'll never know what temperature to target.

## What you SHOULD see

In most cases, there's only one visual indicator that fermentation is happening: bubbles of carbon dioxide passing through your airlock.

Observing a ferment through a clear plastic or glass vessel is interesting, but is not worth the negative effect of light reaching your beer and damaging its flavour. If you do find yourself using a clear vessel, keep it covered with thick cardboard (such as the box it came in), and resist the urge to lift the lid and expose it to light.

# What you WON'T see: the stages of fermentation

**LAG PHASE**

For the first 24 hours after pitching your yeast, it will be absorbing the oxygen you so generously agitated into the beer, as well as minerals and amino acids from the wort. All this nutrition will be used to make new yeast cells. This part of the ferment is called the 'lag phase'. During this time you won't see any activity in the form of bubbles through the airlock.

**EXPONENTIAL GROWTH PHASE**

As the nutrition is fully absorbed, the yeast cells begin to multiply. They have an innate ability to identify the concentration of sugar around them, and in conjunction with a sense of their own concentration of cells, determine how much replication is needed to colonise the wort and consume the sugar. On average, the population of yeast cells will increase five-fold during this time.

In the early part of this phase of exponential growth — at about 24 hours from when yeast was pitched — you will begin to see the occasional bubble push through your airlock. As the cells reproduce and the population nears a sufficient level to fully ferment the beer, some cells will convert over from reproduction to consumption, and the first bits of carbon dioxide and alcohol will be created. As the pressure inside the fermenter builds, it will eventually push bubbles through the airlock, giving you the first visual indication of fermentation.

During the exponential growth phase, the sugars are consumed, and most of the high alcohols, esters and sulfur compounds are being created. Much of these are considered 'off' flavours, or flavour-negative compounds — but don't worry, nature has solved this problem for us. Our yeast, since it is well loved and happy, will reward us and turn this 'green beer' into a mature and tasty drop.

**STATIONARY PHASE**

At this point in the ferment, when the yeast has consumed nearly all the fermentable sugar, it enters the stationary phase. Those yeast cells that aren't chowing down on the last of the sugar switch over to maturing

**What if you don't see any bubbling? Be patient. You may have used an older packet of yeast that contained a number of cells that didn't reactivate. In this case, your alive cells have to multiply a little more before moving to the next phase of the ferment. Or perhaps you targeted a higher ABV beer with a lot of fermentables. In this case, even a fresh, healthy packet of yeast may need more time to grow.**

your beer — a process whereby the yeast cells go back through and absorb some of the compounds they originally excreted, naturally turning them into the pleasant flavour compounds we come to expect in our beer.

For most normal strength ales, this phase runs for 7–10 days from when yeast was pitched, but it can run much longer with higher alcohol ales, warm fermented ales like saisons, and lagers. With a warm fermented beer or a bigger beer, there are more flavour and alcohol compounds created by the yeast that need to be cleaned up. And yeast strains like lager work best at lower temperatures, where they naturally work slower — letting a lager strain work at warm temperatures in the hope of accelerating this process creates more off flavours, so just be patient when using lager strains. Remember, time is a key ingredient in lager — there's no substitute.

## THE END OF FERMENTATION: WHAT NOW?

Fermentation is a like a house party. It starts slow as people get warmed up, but quickly grows as people arrive, the volume gets turned up, the dancing starts, body temperatures rise, drinks are spilled, and the energy increases to where you think the roof might blow off.

Then, when all but the last few drops of beer are gone, and people are exhausted, the energy drops, the body temperatures return to normal, and people start fading away, leaving the host and a few loyal friends to clean up.

When targeting an ABV over 6% consider using two packets of yeast. More yeast isn't always better, so resist the urge to add more until looking into this yourself. (If you want to learn more, read an excellent book by Chris White and Jamil Zainasheff, appropriately called *Yeast: The Practical Guide to Beer Fermentation*.)

### Inside your fermenter

It's now about Day 10 of the fermentation, and you probably see a bubble only once every few minutes at most. The yeast is winding down now, and those infrequent bubbles aren't from active fermentation, but from $CO_2$ that was dissolved in the beer finally rising to the surface and venting off. The yeast will be nearly done with its clean-up. A few vigorous cells may still be chewing on a few larger, harder-to-ferment sugar molecules — but most of the population, realising their work is done, will call it a day and progress into their hibernation stage.

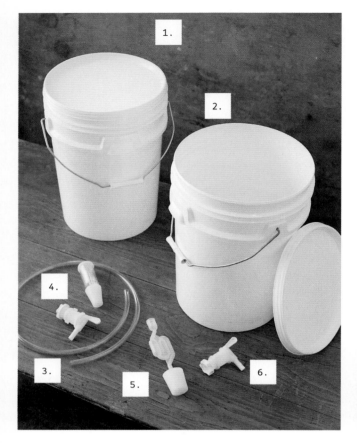

1. Fermenter full of mature beer
2. Secondary maturation vessel bottling bucket, a replica of the fermenter with lid and tap
3. Hose
4. Tap + airlock (will be fitted to your fermenter of beer)
5. Airlock for secondary maturation vessel/bottling bucket
6. Tap for secondary maturation vessel/bottling bucket

Ensure the hose fills with sanitiser, and no air bubbles are trapped within it

In the stationary phase, as they cleaned up the beer after the initial wild party of the exponential growth phase, the cells will have absorbed the nutrients they need to survive in the now nutrient-deficient, high-alcohol environment they created for themselves in anticipation of their next ferment. They will also collide with other cells and clump together, and their collective weight will enable gravity to pull the cells to the bottom of the vessel — a process called 'flocculation'. At the end of this period of 'maturation' — which in the case of your first beer will be around Day 14 — your beer is ready for bottling or kegging.

**Of course, you can mature your beer longer — in a secondary maturation vessel**

Sometimes you need more time to mature your beer, and sometimes life gets in the way and you can't bottle your beer after the allotted 14 days. That's fine, but for the best flavour, we want to 'rack' (the brewing term for moving beer from one vessel to another) your beer off the flocculated yeast and into a new vessel.

When yeast is pitched into wort, some of the cells will be dead, or will die very soon from the stress of the new environment. There's no sadness here, yeast cells die every day, and you've added billions to your wort in anticipation of losing a few. Gravity will pull those cells to the bottom of your fermenter.

In addition to the dead cells that fell out of suspension early on in the ferment, you will also have a dense cake of flocculated live yeast. But they won't stay alive forever. They will begin to exhaust the nutrients they've absorbed for their hibernation and die. Others will die because of the high alcohol level of the now fermented beer. In a perfect world (as in a commercial brewery) you would get those cells out of your fermenter, because they will eventually rupture and spill their 'off' flavoured contents into your beer — a process called **autolysis** (see page 158). Some of this is unavoidable because of the simple design (and low cost) of our home-brewing equipment, and as long as we can keep it to a minimum, the off flavours will not amount to a level detectable to the average person's palate.

A general rule of thumb is to rack your beer no more than 7 days after the airlock stops bubbling. Even if you can't package the beer by this time, or don't want to, it's still good to get the beer off the yeast.

## Racking your beer

To do this, you will need:

- vinyl hosing that fits the end of the tap on your fermenter
- your bucket (second plastic fermenter), with lid and tap
- a second airlock and rubber stopper
- home-brew detergent to clean the equipment
- sanitiser to sanitise the equipment.

The process for sanitising your clean secondary maturation vessel is the same as for your primary fermenter.

→ Ensure all your equipment is clean.
  - Use your detergent to clean the inside workings of the tap.
  - Soak your hosing in detergent and rinse thoroughly.

  - Clean any visible matter from the bucket and airlock.

→ Fix the tap to the bucket.

→ Begin filling the bucket with cool water, and check the tap for leaks.

→ Put the hose, airlock and stopper and lid in the bucket.

→ Add your sanitiser as the water is still filling the bucket.

→ Leave to soak for 20 minutes.

→ Drain the sanitiser.

→ Put the lid, top down, on your sanitised benchtop, and place the other equipment on it.

→ Finish draining the bucket, close the tap, and turn the bucket upside down on top of the lid, covering the other equipment.

**The process of racking (transferring) your beer to a new vessel needs to be done slowly and with care. One day you might graduate to equipment that gives you access to carbon dioxide to protect your beer from oxidation, the great beer staler — but for now we move slow and carefully and do our best not to agitate the beer and absorb excessive oxygen. And the small amount of yeast we still have in suspension will help mitigate against oxidation.**

→ Carefully, so you don't disturb the yeast and other sediment you're trying to rack your beer off, place your fermenter on a benchtop. Disturbing the yeast will send it back into solution, where it will be transferred to your new vessel. Some yeast will end up getting pulled across — don't stress. It's the cells at the bottom of the yeast cake that will fall out of suspension first, and are at highest risk of causing 'off' flavours. Luckily, they're safely tucked away at the bottom of the yeast cake.

→ Put your sanitised secondary maturation vessel on a chair below your fermenter.
- It should be high enough that the transfer hose can reach from the tap of the fermenter to the bottom of the secondary maturation vessel, and low enough that the top of the secondary maturation vessel is below the bottom of the fermenter. This will allow gravity to do its thing.
- Having the hose reach the bottom of the vessel will limit the amount of agitation and oxygen that gets dissolved into your beer. Unlike when adding our wort before pitching our yeast, here we want to limit — or even eliminate — the absorption of oxygen.

→ Ensure the tap on the secondary maturation vessel is closed.

→ Gently ease the rubber stopper out of the hole in the fermenter lid. If you miss this step, and open the tap to start the transfer, you will suck the water from within your airlock into your beer — a major contamination risk (and just gross).

→ Open the tap and allow the beer to flow across.
- When opening the tap, hold the end of the hose to the bottom of the secondary maturation vessel, to reduce the agitation of the beer. Hold the hose there until the end of the hose is submerged in beer; this will limit oxygen pick-up from agitation.
- Having the tap positioned near, but not at the absolute bottom, of the fermenter, means you should be pulling clean beer from above the yeast cake. As mentioned, some yeast will be pulled into suspension by even the gentlest of beer flow, but this shouldn't be more than a light dusting. If your yeast cake is large enough to be pulled through, gently tilt the fermenter back to encourage the yeast to drift away from the tap.
- If your tap was added too low, and constantly pulls yeast through, consider buying a new bucket to act as your fermenter and using the one with the low tap as a dedicated bottling bucket or secondary maturation vessel. In your bottling bucket you will not have a yeast cake to contend with, so the tap can be placed much lower than in a fermenter.

→ When the racking is complete, put your lid on the secondary maturation vessel and affix the stopper and airlock.

→ Fill the airlock with the required amount of water.

→ Move the vessel to the same place you stored it during fermentation, and apply the same effort to maintaining a cool and constant temperature as you did during the initial ferment. The maturation process will not build the same level of heat as the fermenting process, so it shouldn't take as much effort.

# Maturing your beer

At this point, your yeast has done most of its work, and your recipe or intuition are telling you to let your beer sit for another week or more to allow the yeast still in suspension to continue to evolve the flavour of your beer. This can be done for a few days, or for months, depending on the ingredients you used and the flavour you're trying to develop. Throughout this process it's a good idea to taste the beer from time to time to build an inventory of taste memories, and understand how time and temperature improve your beer and to know when it's done. When is it done? It's done when it tastes how you want or when it is no longer changing, whichever comes first.

When tasting, however, remember to temporarily remove the airlock, to avoid creating a vacuum pulling the water from your airlock into your vessel. Also be aware that each time you take liquid out to taste, you're pulling air in — and air (oxygen) is the great enemy of beer. Oxidised malt tastes of cardboard and loses its vibrancy. Air also contains bacteria, which could latch onto any unfermented sugar and create off flavours; the likelihood of this isn't great, as bacteria will struggle in a nutrient-deficient, high-alcohol environment, but it's still a risk. So taste carefully knowing the risks.

The time it takes for a beer to properly mature is something you can only learn from experience. And like raising a kid, you won't know if you made the right decision until it's too late to make a change! But here are some general rules of thumb with the number of days from when the visible signs of fermentation end (when your airlock bubbles once every minute).

- **Pale, amber and brown ales** below around 6% alcohol should generally be allowed to mature for about 7 days from the end of fermentation.
- **Darker beers** with roasted malt additions will benefit from a little more time than paler beers, to allow some of the acrid roast malt particles to fall out of suspension; 14 days from the end of fermentation should do it.

- **Higher alcohol beers**, with over 6% alcohol, need even more time. It's generally a linear scale; the higher the ABV, the more time needed. A 7% beer will benefit from 14 days of maturation from the end of the ferment, while a 10% will need 21 days.
- **Lagers** should be given at least 21 days, or as much as a few months, depending on their alcohol level and grist.
- **Hoppy beers** will start to lose their hop aroma and flavour, so don't stretch your maturations too long. Thankfully a dry hop addition (see below) can be added during maturation, and the yeast and hops will work concurrently to improve the beer's flavour.

The one rule that supersedes all of the above is your own personal preference. Taste the beers as they are maturing, build a flavour memory, and make your decisions on maturation by your own palate and experience. If you think it's ready because it tastes good to you, then it is ready for bottling or kegging.

## Turn up the volume: now it gets really exciting!

It's in the process of fermentation, and the subsequent maturation, that yeast creates and refines flavour. But the flavour of your beer isn't limited to what the yeast will do. It's in this stage of beer making that we, as brewers, can get really creative with the additions we add to our fermenter.

From the traditional practices of 'dry hopping' and adding fruit, to the less traditional and now commonplace additions like cacao and coffee, the culinary world is at your disposal. Find inspiration from wherever you like, but keep in mind what yeast might do to that ingredient, and think about whether it's best added with lots of yeast in the primary fermenter, or with much less yeast in the secondary maturation vessel.

### DRY HOPPING

We've discussed at length what happens when hops are added to the kettle — early additions for bittering, later additions for flavour, and additions at the very end for aroma. 'Dry hopping' is the practice of

## Fruit fizzers

When it comes to adding fruit to beers, it's probably easier to list those that don't give good results. I haven't been able to make bananas work. Strawberries, as shown here, are commonly used, but add little value; all the flavour seems to be in the sugar, which when the yeast ferments leaves nothing.

Wine grapes are good, but the grapes sold in grocery stores are a waste, as they leave no flavour.

Apples are another commonly used fruit I've never made work. Ciders require unique apples that don't taste good to eat and aren't sold in grocery stores. And fermented apple juice thins out a beer, making it bland. If you have access to cider apples, give them a try and see if you like the result!

adding hops to the fermenting, or fermented, beer for additional hop aroma and flavour.

The best place to add dry hops is when the yeast is finished fermenting and is entering the maturation stage. At this point, around Day 7, most of the yeast is done and is settling to the bottom of the fermenter. Because adding hops requires opening the fermenter and exposing the beer to oxygen, it's best to dry hop when there is still a bit of yeast floating around, because it will scavenge up that oxygen. And waiting until the fermentation is complete means the volatile hop aromas you're trying to add won't be volatised off by the agitation and bubbling of an active ferment.

Some brewers detect a better result from adding dry hops to beer after the yeast has been separated. The thought here is that the yeast will take some of the dry hop flavour with it, if the hops are added while the yeast is still in the beer.

Brewers wanting to use finings to clarify their beer will also benefit from using the finings and separating the yeast from the beer before dry hopping, as the hops may interfere with the action of the finings. **A note of caution** when using finings: as they are very effective in removing yeast, you may end up with insufficient yeast in suspension to bottle-condition the beer. Only use finings if you intend to force-carbonate in a keg, or are prepared and skilled enough to introduce fresh yeast prior to bottling.

## EXPERIMENTING WITH FRUIT

Most fruits, if not all, will have fermentable sugar readily available. When you add fruit to beer in the presence of yeast, you will create conditions for yeast to kick off a second fermentation.

It's important for this second ferment to occur when it's in your fermenter and under control so the carbon dioxide can vent off. If you add the fruit close to bottling, and the second ferment happens in your bottles, you run the risk of over-pressurising the bottles — the scary part of this is that the glass will give before the crown seal, so you are effectively making **glass grenades**. No, I'm not over dramatising it. **This is a real risk — take it seriously!**

Thankfully, the risk is easy to avoid. Prepare your fruit and add it when there is:

1) plenty of yeast still in suspension, and

2) the beer is still warm enough to encourage the yeast to start fermenting.

And give the beer enough time to re-ferment. Watch the airlock for the visual cues discussed above.

The easiest and safest fruit to work with is frozen. Regulations vary by country, but generally frozen fruit is chilled down to −18°C (0°F). At that temperature, the wild yeast living on the fruit will be killed or highly degraded, so it's unlikely to activate in your beer and affect the flavour. At that temperature, the cell walls of the fruit are also damaged, so they'll rupture more quickly in your beer and release the flavours and sugar of the fruit.

**Fresh fruit** is a great option, particularly when you can get imperfect fruit from a farmer at little or no cost. Consumers these days are trained to want beautiful, perfectly shaped fruit with no bruises — but when it's going to be peeled, sliced, mashed and added to beer, none of that matters. Ask the growers at your local farmers' market what they do with their imperfect fruit — I bet they'll be happy to share a kilo with you in exchange for a bottle of your beer.

Fresh fruit hasn't used high amounts of electricity to freeze and store, and when purchased locally, it also hasn't used diesel to move it around the world, so it has significant environmental benefits. But on the downside, it hasn't had the cellular degradation or sterilisation of the freezing process, and it requires you to cut it up in a sanitary way.

Sourcing fruit very much depends on what is grown near you, versus the cost and environmental impact of shipping it to you. Don't just look at the price per kilo — remember the 'externalities' that don't appear in the price, but are a real cost to our environment, or the person in the country that grew them.

I personally find fresh **stone fruits** contribute wonderful flavour fairly quickly, and are cost effective and relatively easy to handle. If using berries, frozen ones tend to be the better option, as fresh berries can cost a fortune, and their thick cell walls benefit from the freezing process. If you're lucky enough to live in a berry-growing region, try freezing fresh ones at home for a week or two before using them.

Other excellent fruits include **watermelon**, **cucumber** (yep, it's a fruit!), **currants**, **mango**, **citrus** (both the peel and the juice), **cherries** and **figs**.

Think about the fruit and how you access its flavour, and what flavour it might contribute. Process the fruit accordingly — for example, the pith of citrus fruit isn't pleasant to eat, so keep that out of your beer. And the rind of a watermelon has nothing to offer, so cut that off and just add the good stuff. At super-high levels of consumption, some pits and seeds are actually dangerous, so do some research and use your judgment.

## ADDING COFFEE, CHOCOLATE, HERBS

Ingredients that won't ferment should be added after the yeast is removed. And ingredients that might overwhelm the flavour of your beer should be added at a time when they can be separated from the beer, to lock in the amount of flavour they contribute.

**Cacao nibs**, for instance, need a fair bit of contact time with the beer. Because of this, you don't want yeast in there that might autolyse*, contributing a negative flavour to your beer.

For those ingredients that need a longer contact time to impart their flavour, it's important to get the beer transferred off the yeast before adding them.

Intensely **aromatic herbs** can quickly overpower your beer, so try adding them just a couple of days before you plan to rack or bottle your beer, so they can be separated when the flavour gets to where you want it — or add them in a sanitised bag that can be removed.

**Coffee beans** — whole, cracked or ground — add excellent flavour and complexity to beer. In each form you get a different

**\* Autolysis is the process of yeast cells dying and rupturing, spilling unwanted flavours of meat and burned rubber into your beer. All yeast will autolyse eventually, though the process will be slowed by keeping the temperature of the beer low and constant. The best way to avoid these flavours is to rack the beer off the yeast before autolysis begins to occur.**

attribute of the bean. And experimenting with different roasts can add another layer of complexity. Like herbs, the beans can be added two or three days before racking the beer. You can also make a very strong coffee in a plunger and add that straight to the fermenter.

**A NOTE ON SANITATION**

At this stage of the process you have alcohol and very little fermentable sugar, making your beer hostile to wild yeast and bacteria, which are therefore unlikely to ruin the flavour of your beer.

However, everything you add at this stage introduces a risk of infection. Few, if any, hops, fruits, herbs and spices can be properly sanitised without destroying their flavour — but don't let the risk of contamination stop you from experimenting.

Be sure to sanitise your bags, cutting boards, jars or any equipment you use to process and handle the addition. In the high-alcohol, low-nutrient environment of finished beer, any yeast or bacteria that does get in will have a very subtle and slow flavour impact that you may not even detect unless you store the beer for months in a warm environment; keeping it cold will limit bacterial growth.

# Cold maturation

As home brewers, we're at the mercy of the ambient temperature we happen to be living in, but provided the temperature in the fermenter is not much over 22°C (72°F), in most cases we can still make some beautiful-tasting beers.

If you can cool the beer, when the yeast is completely finished with its maturation process, you will get the benefits of additional clarification and flavour development. The cold encourages the yeast flocculation process, leaving you with a clearer beer more quickly than with a warm maturation. And some yeast strains, notably those used to make lager, will continue their work at temperatures as low as 0°C (32°F), further improving the beer flavour.

The downside of a cold maturation is you can't then bottle-condition without the complicated process of adding back more yeast. While I do encourage you to move toward this process of cold maturation, don't be in a rush, and only do so when you're kegging and force-carbonating, or are confident enough to properly add back the right amount of healthy yeast.

Now that we're done fermenting and maturing our beer, it's time to bottle or keg it!

# Packaging + Conditioning

You now have about 19 litres (5 gallons) of beautifully fermented and matured home-made beer. The only things standing between you and the pride of watching your friends and family smile as they take a sip are getting bubbles into the beer, and putting the beer into something they can drink it from.

These two processes are called conditioning and packaging, and while they rarely get any glory, they are the unsung heroes of the brewing process. Cut a corner and get these wrong, and all your time, effort, money and patience will be for nothing.

**Packaging** is the process of racking your beer into a serving vessel. In the case of home brewing, we're talking about bottles or kegs.

Bottles are cheap, can be taken to parties and competitions, and can be stored anywhere cool and dark — but they're a challenge to clean and sanitise, tedious to fill, need to sit for two weeks before drinking, and are subject to domino-style catastrophic spills.

Kegs are easy to clean, easy to fill, and easy to carbonate — but require hundreds of dollars and a dedicated fridge, and you can't easily take a six-pack equivalent volume to your friend's place for dinner or the game. So for now, start with bottles, and start putting your loose change into a piggy bank to buy a draft system one day.

**Conditioning** is the process of putting bubbles in your beer. Naturally carbonating your beer in the bottle is called 'bottle conditioning', and the yeast does the work. As long as you have yeast in the beer, feed it a small but very specific quantity of sugar, and seal the vessel, you don't have to do much more than store it at a good fermentation temperature and wait. The process of injecting bubbles into your beer is called 'force carbonation', and is one option available when using a keg; the other option is **natural conditioning**, in which the keg is essentially one giant bottle.

## Bottling your beer

With your first batch of beer, and most of the others that will follow, it will be two weeks since you brewed your beer and you're ready to rack it off the yeast, 'prime' it with a small addition of sugar, and get it into your bottles. The bottles will then need to be sealed, so the gas that is subsequently created is trapped and, as the pressure builds, absorbed into the beer.

Before we do all this, we're going to ensure our bottles are clean, then we'll sanitise them, and prepare our priming sugar. We'll rack the beer off our yeast and maturation sediment, straight into the bottling bucket with the priming sugar. We'll then fill and cap each bottle, and store them to let the yeast once again do its thing — before we can chill them, pour them, analyse them and enjoy them.

**WHAT YOU NEED**

- Bottle brush
- Bottle rinser (optional, but recommended)
- Bottle tree, for draining the sanitised bottles (optional)
- Vinyl transfer hose, for racking
- Enough brown crown-seal glass bottles for 19 litres (5 gallons) of beer, plus a few extra just in case
- Bottling bucket and lid
- An additional clean bucket or tub for sanitising the bottles
- Bottle-filling wand
- Bottle capper
- Bottle caps
- A small pot with a lid, for sanitising the priming sugar
- A larger pot with a lid, for sterilising the bottle caps
- Priming sugar
- Sanitiser
- Home-brew detergent
- Your beautifully fermented, mature beer
- Beer, for drinking!

## WHAT YOU NEED TO DO

→ Put 250 ml (9 fl oz/1 cup) of water in your small pot, put a lid on it, and bring it to a boil. (We want the lid on, to sterilise it.)

→ When the water is boiling, turn off the heat and add your carefully measured priming sugar, stirring to dissolve it. Do not add more sugar than directed for your recipe. If you have more or less water than the intended 19 litres (5 gallons), adjust your sugar accordingly, and precisely. Over-priming your beer will lead to excessive $CO_2$ production and pressure in the bottle, which may result in:

- slightly over-carbonated beer that tingles too much when drinking it, distracting you from its flavour
- significantly over-carbonated beer that gushes uncontrollably out of the bottle when it's opened
- **dangerously overcarbonated beer that bursts bottles!**

→ Let the pot cool on its own, or in a small water bath, while you run through the next steps.

→ Sip your beer! At this stage, the risk of personal injury is minimal, unless you're just naturally accident prone — in which case maybe don't sip that beer. You can still mess things up, so enjoy your beer in moderation.

→ Clean your bottles of any visible yeast sediment or debris using a home-brew detergent and bottle brush.

→ Rinse the bottles thoroughly with the hottest water you can handle — any detergent residue remaining on the bottle will degrade your beer foam, and may affect your yeast's ability to condition the beer.

→ Sanitise your clean bottles, bottling bucket (with the tap properly fixed), lid, vinyl hose and disassembled bottle-filling wand by placing them in your bottling bucket and the extra tub, filling each bucket with water and adding your sanitiser.

- Run some sanitiser through the tap.
- Check the tap for leaks.
- Make sure each bottle sits upright and is held down to fully fill with sanitiser. And make sure the sanitiser is added and mixed in before the bottle fills, so it isn't just water that fills the bottles —

you need each bottle filled with properly mixed
sanitiser, and no air.

- One trick for filling the bottles faster is to insert
  your bottle-filling wand into the empty bottle, so air
  can escape the bottle as it is filled with the sanitiser
  and water.

→ Leave to soak for 20 minutes, or as specified by the
sanitiser manufacturer.

→ Meanwhile, sip that beer again — it's a bit warmer
now, and your perception of its flavour will be changing
as it degasses and the aroma opens up.

→ In your larger pot, bring a couple of litres of water
nearly to a boil.

- When the water is nearly at a boil, turn off the heat,
  then add enough bottle caps to seal your bottles,
  plus a few extras. You don't want to boil your caps,

## Magic trick #4: Drink and rinse

Cleaning dried yeast sediment out of the bottom of a beer bottle is mind-numbingly
frustrating. To avoid having to do it at all, care for your bottles as soon as you've finished
drinking from them — rather than just before filling them.

When enjoying a home brew, pour the contents of your bottle into your glass, and
before you walk away to enjoy it, rinse the bottle thoroughly with the hottest water your
hands can tolerate. Pour some water into the bottle, cover it with your hand and shake it
to dislodge the yeast from the bottom. Pour the yeasty water out and repeat until the water
coming out has no sign of yeast — two or three rinses is usually enough.

Store the bottle upside down in a clean six-pack carton or beer crate until your next
bottling day, when it should be ready to go straight into sanitiser — no cleaning!

but adding them to near-boiling water will make sure they're adequately sanitised.

- Let the caps soak for the time being.

→ Drain each bottle and invert them, so they continue to drain.

- A bottle tree is a handy purchase for this process. It safely holds the bottles inverted and avoids the potential domino effect of storing 30–60 inverted, top-heavy bottles.

→ Drain the bottling bucket through the tap.

→ Place the lid, top down, on a sanitised bench.

→ Remove and drain the hose, and place it on the lid.

→ Remove the bottle-filling wand parts, reassemble it, and place it on the lid.

→ Pour out any remaining sanitiser, close the tap, invert the bottling bucket, and place it on the lid, covering the other equipment.

→ Check that your priming sugar solution is warm to the touch.

- It's not vital that this solution be any specific temperature. The relatively small volume will have little or no impact when blended with 19 litres (5 gallons) of finished beer. That said, we don't want it boiling — warm to the touch is cool enough. Give it more time to cool if needed.

→ Carefully, so you don't disturb the yeast and/or sediment you're trying to rack your beer off, place your fermenter on a benchtop.

- After a standard two-week fermentation and maturation, there will be enough yeast still in suspension to re-ferment in the bottle, so try to minimise how much yeast you agitate back into suspension. Some yeast from the bottom of the fermenter will get transferred across — don't stress, it's unavoidable and won't cause any harm.

→ Drain the water from your pot of caps and leave the lid on to protect them from dust and bacteria.

→ Turn your sanitised and drained bottling bucket right-side-up, and ensure (again) that the tap is closed — we are way too far down the process to spill finished beer on the floor!

→ Put your sanitised bottling bucket on a chair below your fermenter.

- It should be high enough that the transfer hose can reach from the tap of the fermenter to the bottom of the bottling bucket; and low enough that the top of the bottling bucket is below the bottom of the fermenter. This will allow gravity to do its thing.

- Having the hose reach the bottom of the bottling bucket will limit the amount of agitation and oxygen that gets splashed into your beer. Introducing too much oxygen at this stage will stale your beer.

→ Pour your cooled priming solution into the bottling bucket.

→ Attach one end of the hose to the fermenter tap.

→ Hold the other end of the hose to the bottom of the bottling bucket, to reduce the agitation of the beer as it flows into the bottling bucket.

→ Open the fermenter tap and allow the beer to start flowing across. Hold the hose at the bottom of the bottling bucket until the end of the hose is submerged in beer; this will limit oxygen pickup from agitation.

- The flow of beer into the bottling bucket will adequately and uniformly mix the priming solution into the beer.
- If your fermenter tap is at the right height, you should be pulling clean beer from above the yeast cake at the bottom of the fermenter. As mentioned earlier, some yeast will be pulled into suspension by even the gentlest of beer flow, but this shouldn't be more than a light dusting. If your yeast cake is being pulled through the tap, gently tilt the fermenter back to encourage the yeast to drift away from the tap.

→ When the beer has finished racking, rest the lid of the bottling bucket on top of the bottling bucket.

- The lid is helpful to limit dust and debris falling into your now sugar-rich beer.
- No airlock is needed on the lid, as that will create a seal as we drain the beer from the bottling bucket into bottles.

→ Move the empty fermenter aside, and carefully place the now full bottling bucket where the fermenter was.

→ Move the hose from the fermenter to the bottling bucket tap, then fix the bottle-filling wand to the other end.

→ Take a bottle off the tree, insert the wand into the bottle, open the tap on the bottling bucket, and press the wand down into the bottom of the bottle to disengage the seal and start the flow of beer.

→ As the flow reaches the top, take the pressure off the wand to stop the flow of beer, being careful to not overflow the bottle. You want the fill level to reach the absolute top of the bottle.

→ As you remove the wand, the displacement it produced will reduce the fill level of the beer to about 3 cm (1¼ inches) from the top — this is the perfect fill level.

- Any less and there will be too much oxygen-filled 'headspace' (space at the top of the bottle) that will stale the beer.
- Any more and you risk over-pressurising the bottle during the re-ferment, which may cause it to explode.

→ Place a cap on the bottle and seal it using the bottle capper.

→ Place the capped bottle in an old six-pack holder or beer crate to reduce the risk of a domino-style mess.

→ When you've finished capping all the bottles, store them in the same spot your fermenter was — somewhere dark, out of the way, and around 19°C (66°F).

→ In a week, put one of your bottles of beer in the fridge for a few hours. Chilling the beer will help the gas absorb into the beer, and encourage any yeast still in suspension to settle on the bottom of the bottle. Once chilled, crack it open, pour it into a glass, and give it a taste.
  - If the gas level is good, the beer is done. Congrats!

- What is a 'good' gas level? It should be enough that your beer pours and creates foam. (No foam could mean a number of things, so if you don't have foam, but see gas bubbles rising in the beer, refer to the evaluation and trouble-shooting section in chapter 7.)
- Another indicator of 'good' is a small smoke-like cloud in the headspace of the bottle immediately after you pop the top.
- Remember that 'good' is subjective, and depends on the beer style (if you're concerned with accurately representing a style). Carbon dioxide in beer has an impact on beer flavour — so much so that it can almost be considered a flavour. The same beer served flat, carbonated, and highly carbonated will taste remarkably different, and it's up to each brewer to decide how they want their beer to taste. So do some research, work by trial and error, and decide for yourself what is a 'good' level of carbonation.
- If you don't have a 'good' gas level, wait another week and test one more bottle. Repeat this testing until they're ready.

→ Generally, after two weeks, your beer is ready to evaluate and enjoy!

# Cap that!

My girlfriend, now wife, helped me on my first bottling day by running the capper. I filled each bottle, put a cap on it and handed it to her to crimp with the bottle-capper — the perfect team. Two weeks later, there were no bubbles in the beer: the caps weren't on tight enough and all the gas had seeped out! Trying not to take my disappointment out on her — the most beautiful woman I've ever met, I might add — I took a gamble and moved the height setting on the capper down one notch and resealed each bottle.

Luckily, there was still enough re-fermentation occurring, and a week later, nature decided I should marry her by rewarding me with perfectly carbonated beer. Moral of the story: check your equipment, and don't stress — beer is actually a lot more forgiving than we sometimes think.

## Kegging your beer

There comes a point in every home-brewer's life when they have cleaned and sanitised their last bottle. When you've reached that point, and are prepared to spend the money, you will be welcomed with open arms into the world of draft beer.

But when it comes to kegging, don't think you're getting off easy. Forced carbonation can be straightforward and easy, but it can also be frustratingly slow.

**WHAT YOU NEED**
- Corny keg*
- Keg/carboy brush (for cleaning)
- Keg gas fitting
- Keg tap
- $CO_2$ cylinder
- $CO_2$ regulator
- Refrigerator

**\* A corny keg is one of the tall, thin, metal vessels that soft drink companies use to distribute the syrups for their post-mix systems. They are simple to use, have a big opening for cleaning, and are widely available, so home brewers have adopted them. You will find these for sale at your local home-brew shop.**

**WHAT YOU NEED TO DO**

Before filling your keg, you need to properly clean and sanitise it, as you would a fermenter or bottle, by filling it with water and adding your sanitiser. Make sure the dispensing tube, that reaches to the bottom of the keg, is flushed out during cleaning, and filled with sanitiser when sanitising. It's a sealed tube that won't naturally fill on its own, so to do this, press the valve piece in the centre of the 'out' valve, to crack the seal and allow it to fill. Make sure the cap of the corny keg is positioned in the keg, and that it, and the gasket, are soaking in the sanitiser.

After the 20-minute soak is finished, put the seal back on the cap and secure it in the opening. Clamp the cap into place.

Connect your gas line to your $CO_2$ regulator, and your regulator to your $CO_2$ cylinder. Ensure the regulator is loosened and set to zero pressure. Open the gas cylinder, turn the regulator knob to 1–2 PSI and listen for leaks. Correct any leaks in the gas line fitting or where the regulator attaches to the gas bottle. Attach the gas line, using the corny keg fitting, to the 'in' valve on the corny keg. You should hear gas flowing into the keg. Check the keg for leaks where the cap is fitted.

Fix your keg tap to the 'out' valve, point the tap down a drain, and open the tap. The sanitiser will flow out of the tap, and the regulator will allow more gas to flow, forcing the sanitiser out of the keg and filling the keg with $CO_2$.

When the sanitiser is fully drained, close the tap and let the keg fully pressurise — you'll know this is done when the regulator stops hissing. You now have a sanitised keg that is fully purged of oxygen and ready to be filled with beer.

The laws of physics mean you can't use gravity to move beer into a sealed and pressurised keg, so you have to vent the pressure from the keg using the valve on top of the keg or the tap. Once the pressure is gone, crack the lid open. Using a sanitised hose, rack the beer from the fermenter into the keg, just as you would rack beer into your bottling bucket. Don't overfill the keg, just as you wouldn't overfill a bottle.

Seal the keg and attach the keg gas fitting from the regulator to the keg. Adjust the regulator to put 1–2 PSI into the headspace. Check for pressure leaks. If there are leaks, vent the pressure, remove the lid and try resealing it. Add pressure and check again. Corny kegs are usually sold second-hand, and the lids sometimes are a little finicky — so keep opening the lid and trying again; it will eventually work. Put a little more pressure in the keg if after a couple of attempts it's not sealing well; sometimes the added pressure helps force the cap into its seat. Once it's sealed, put the beer in your beer fridge. You are now ready to force carbonate your beer.

Force-carbonating your beer takes time and patience, despite the haste its name implies.

Done properly, force-carbonating will take 24–48 hours, depending on how cold the beer is and how often you're able to check on it. The process involves slowly adding more and more head pressure to the beer as the $CO_2$ dissolves. To understand what you need to do, you need to understand the physics happening in your keg.

There is beer in your keg, and some space above it called the headspace. As you add gas pressure to the keg through the gas portal, you're increasing the pressure of the headspace. That headspace pressure is being forced down on the surface of the beer, and the $CO_2$ will be absorbed into the beer, until the gas in the beer accumulates to create an equal amount of pressure to that in the headspace — this is an 'equilibrium', where the headspace and beer pressures are exactly equal. This takes time to occur, and is expedited by cooling the beer. As a home brewer, you never actually know the pressure of the beer, just that of the headspace, as reported back by the regulator. So you are constantly making intuitive guesses about how many volumes of $CO_2$ are in the beer.

If you have all the time in the world, you will put your keg and gas bottle in the fridge. Connect the regulator and set the pressure to your desired amount, given the beer temperature, and your required volumes of $CO_2$, and wait for the whole system to come to equilibrium. As the beer absorbs gas, the regulator will allow more gas to flow. When the beer has absorbed as much pressure as the regulator is set to, the system will be in balance and the regulator will stop letting gas into the keg. This will probably take a few days, if not a week.

A slightly faster method is to set your regulator to a higher pressure than you need, based on the temperature of your beer and your desired volumes

of $CO_2$, and shake the keg. As you shake it, you're increasing the surface area of beer exposed to gas, and making small bubbles in the beer that are more readily dissolvable. After you have shaken the keg for 30 seconds to a minute, let it rest for 3 hours, before repeating the process two more times. The risk with this process is that you end up over-carbonating your beer, making it difficult to pour and creating waste.

How do you know what pressure to set the regulator to? That depends on the temperature of your beer (those stick-on thermometers work on kegs as well), and the level of carbonation you want. Most ales are packaged around at 2.5 volumes of $CO_2$ (what's a volume? A unit of measure: 2.5 volumes in one litre of beer means you have 2.5 litres of $CO_2$ disolved in that one litre). That's a great place to start. Volumes of $CO_2$ are a function of temperature and pressure. At a colder beer temperature, a relatively lower pressure is needed to achieve the same volumes of $CO_2$ in the beer that a warmer beer temperature would require. In order to

properly set your $CO_2$ regulator, you'll need to know the temperature of your beer and consult a chart or online $CO_2$ beer calculator (which would be a digital version of the data in the chart).

To check the level of $CO_2$ in your beer, you'll need to pour a sample. There are no better scientific tools, that a homebrewer can afford, than your eyes and tastebuds. To check your kegged beer's $CO_2$ level, and to subsequently pour and enjoy that beer, you'll need the following:

- a keg of beer
- gas bottle and regulator
- gas line and gas fitting
- beer tap and fitting
- a glass.

→ Vent the keg by lifting the release value on the keg.

→ Connect your regulator to your gas bottle and turn on the bottle.

→ Set your regulator to about 3 PSI — since you're just giving the keg enough pressure to push out the beer, you don't need anywhere near as much pressure as when you were carbonating the beer.

→ Open the tap over your beer glass and pour enough beer to get a sense of the foam that's created.
  - If it's too flat, turn the pressure on the regulator up to the PSI setting needed given your beer temperature and desired $CO_2$ levels and let it sit, or use the shake method.
  - If it's just right, enjoy! (At the end of your beer service, up the pressure inside the keg to that which you were carbonating it at, to avoid $CO_2$ coming out of solution until you need to pour a beer.)
  - If it's overcarbonated, vent the pressure in the headspace and wait. The $CO_2$ will eventually escape from the beer until an equilibrium is formed in the headspace — you may have to vent and wait a few times, depending on how far overcarbonated your beer is.

Kegging and force-carbonating beer takes time and patience, but it is worth getting the hang of. Never having to fill another bottle is worth the time and energy. As is having fresh draft beer in your home!

# Advanced techniques

Learning to brew is a modular process. The basics of fermentation and sanitation are the foundation to which all the other modules are attached.

The **hot side** — all those brewing processes before the wort is cooled and bacterial contamination becomes a concern — with its various hop additions, can also be easily expanded from using only malt extract, to using malt extract as a base, and building in layers of flavour and texture from specialty grains.

And the **cold side** — those brewing processes after the wort is cooled, and where sanitation is paramount — has many more permutations from the various yeast strains that affect beer flavour, from their contribution of fruity esters and spicy phenols, to the residual sugar the yeast strains leave in the finished beer.

In this section we'll run through the steps needed to add specialty grain character to your beer, a process not much more complicated than making a large cup of tea.

We'll also discuss how yeast starters are made. Yeast starters, as the name suggests, give your dormant yeast a healthy and gentle awakening, to get it ready for a vigorous and complete ferment. It's a process that requires a few extra pieces of equipment, but I highly recommend it for the benefits it will have on your ferments and the additional beer styles using liquid yeast will unlock for you.

## Extract plus specialty grains

Specialty grains are those that give beer the distinct colour, flavour and texture that help drinkers identify it as a particular style.

Specialty grains, while contributing some fermentable sugars, don't need to be mashed in the same way as all-grain brewers do their base malts,

and will impart their colour and flavour when steeped in the kettle like a teabag, prior to the malt extract being added. They are then removed from the kettle, rinsed with some hot water, and the brewing process continues as for an extract brew.

### THINGS YOU'LL NEED

The extract brewing equipment (see pages 98–105) is pretty much all that's needed.

The additional bits you need are:

- a nylon bag to hold your crushed grains
- a second pot to heat your sparge (rinse) water
- a pasta colander to hold your grains over your kettle as you rinse them.

You may also need a malt mill, if your local home-brew shop doesn't offer a milling service.

### WHAT YOU NEED TO DO

→ Source your grains for the recipe you wish to brew.

→ If your home-brew shop offers a milling service, only have your grains milled if you intend to use them right way — milled grains will quickly stale.

→ Fill your kettle about halfway and put the heat on high. We're looking for a temperature of 65–68°C (149–154°F).

- If it's too hot, you will extract unwanted, harsh-tasting tannins from the grain.
- If it's too cool, the thick syrupy wort won't run through the grains as well as it could, and you'll lose some of the available sugar, flavour and colour.

→ Fill your extra saucepan with water and begin heating it to between 72–78°C (162–172°F).

→ Place your milled grain in your nylon bag and seal it.

→ When your kettle has reached 68°C (154°F), place the grain bag in the kettle. This will cool the wort slightly — keep an eye on the temperature and turn the burner on gently and briefly to maintain it at 64–70°C (147–158°F).

- Any time your burner is on, keep your grain bag away from the bottom of the kettle to avoid scorching it.
- This step can be done in the oven, if it can hold a specific enough temperature, and is large enough to hold your kettle.

→ Maintain the wort temperature at 64–70°C (147–158°F) for 30 minutes.

→ At the end of the 30 minutes, taking care not to burn yourself, carefully lift the grain bag out of the wort and place the pasta colander over the kettle, setting the grain bag in the colander.

→ Using the 72–78°C (162–172°F) water in your extra saucepan, rinse the grains until your kettle is two-thirds to three-quarters full.

- Don't over-rinse your grains. While more rinsing may yield more sugar, you will eventually begin to extract harsh-tasting tannins, just as you will when using water that's too hot.
- Also avoid squeezing your grain bag — you only want what comes out on its own.

→ Bring your kettle to a boil, then continue with the brewing process like you're making an extract beer, following the instructions laid out at the beginning of this chapter.

## Starting your liquid yeast

As a brewer, I hope your own journey leads you to a stage where you can embrace the materials you have around you, to make your own unique flavours.

Ideally, these truly creative beers should have their roots in flavour experiences you've had while tasting traditional beers, building on rather than replicating them, to give a sense of place to where you brewed your beer. But before you set out to create something new, it pays to understand how those traditional styles are made. And one way to really dial into the flavour of a particular style is to use the same strain of yeast as the original beer you're inspired by.

Dried yeast has many advantages, as already discussed, but its main disadvantage is the limited variety offered by the yeast labs that sell it. Many great beers are made with yeast strains that are not available in dry form, so this is where liquid yeast must be used.

Liquid yeast is shipped in a dormant state that is not quite ready to get to work — like most of us without

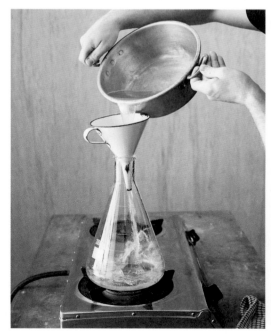

our morning coffee. To get it ready for work, and to maximise your chances of a clean-tasting and complete ferment, we'll brew a small amount of low-gravity wort, to which you'll add your yeast 24–36 hours before it is to be pitched into your home brew.

The small quantity and low gravity are stress-free conditions for your yeast to 'wake up' in.

## THINGS YOU'LL NEED

- 2 litre (70 fl oz) Erlenmeyer flask + small piece of foil + 2 litre bowl, **OR** a 2 litre growler + 2 litre saucepan with lid
- Small funnel
- Thermometer
- Rubber stopper (sized to fit your growler or flask)
- Airlock
- Sanitiser
- 100 g (3½ oz) dried malt extract
- Ice, for an ice bath

## WHAT YOU NEED TO DO

→ Mix up enough sanitiser to submerge your airlock, funnel (if using a growler) and thermometer, then sanitise them.

→ If using a growler, you will also need to sanitise the growler.
- First, ensure it's clean!
- Add 2 ml of iodophor, or the appropriate amount of other sanitiser, and fill the growler with water. Leave to soak for the appropriate time.
- The nice thing about using an Erlenmeyer flask is that it's designed to boil liquids in, and the boiling process will sterilise the vessel, so there's less to clean and sanitise.

→ Add 1 litre (35 fl oz) of water to your flask or saucepan and heat it up to a boil.
- If you're using a saucepan, put the lid on to sanitise it and speed up the process.
- You will boil with the lid off when the malt extract is added — for safety, and so the volatiles will have time to evaporate off.

→ When the water is boiling, remove the flask or saucepan from the heat and add the malt extract, swirling or stirring to dissolve.
- If using a flask, pouring the malt extract into the opening can be a challenge. Instead, carefully pour the boiled water and malt extract into your bowl and stir to combine. Pour the combined mixture back into the flask using your funnel.

→ Place back over a low to medium heat and boil, uncovered, for 10 minutes.
- **Proceed carefully, being mindful of boil-overs!**
- We want to boil and sanitise the wort, but not evaporate off a significant quantity, so adjust your heat to a gentle, but constant, boil.
- If you over-evaporate, you'll have a higher-gravity wort than intended, and the yeast will have a slightly more stressful wake-up.

→ After 10 minutes, remove from the heat. Cover the flask with foil, or the saucepan with the lid.

→ Make an ice bath and cool your wort to 20–22°C (68–72°F), checking the temperature using your sanitised thermometer.
- If it's not cool enough, rinse the thermometer and return it to the sanitiser. Put it back in the ice bath until the wort is at the right temperature.

→ If using a growler and saucepan, empty the growler of sanitiser, then invert it and let it drain.

- Using your sanitised funnel, add the cooled wort from the saucepan to the growler, splashing it to aerate and absorb as much oxygen as possible.

→ If using a flask, carefully (so as to not burn yourself or spill the wort) shake the flask, with your hand securely over the foil covering the opening, to encourage oxygen to dissolve into the wort.

→ Add your yeast to the flask or growler.

→ Covering the flask or growler with the sanitised foil or growler cap, swirl or shake the vessel to encourage more oxygen absorption.

→ Fix your sanitised airlock to the flask or growler using the rubber stopper and set it aside in your favourite fermenting place.

→ During the **next 18 hours**, swirl the vessel from time to time to re-suspend the yeast in solution.

- After this time, the yeast will have consumed the available nutrients.
- Leave the vessel alone and let the yeast settle to the bottom.
- You don't want to leave it any longer than 24 hours. (If life gets in the way and that's not possible, it can sit for 48 hours, but the yeast will begin to hibernate again if you wait too long.)

→ When you're ready to pitch your yeast, decant off about half to three-quarters of the clear wort and discard it.

- If your yeast didn't settle, don't bother decanting, as you will lose some yeast cells.

→ With the remaining starter wort, swirl the vessel to suspend the yeast, then pour it into your cooled and aerated batch of home-brew wort.

→ The starter wort won't taste all that great, but that's not so critical that you need to stress about it. It's a relatively small quantity you'll be adding to a much larger quantity, and it won't have a significant flavour impact.

You won't see much, if any activity, in your airlock during this process, but have faith — the yeast will be absorbing the oxygen and nutrients, and getting prepped to do their best work for you.

## Yeast starters: are they really necessary?

There is some debate around whether a yeast starter is actually necessary. If you have very fresh yeast that didn't travel long or far, and you're brewing a beer that's 5% alcohol or less, you can get away without one. That said, provided you use excellent hygiene, there is no downside to doing one.

But if you have old yeast, or it was shipped from overseas (possibly across the Equator in a box with couple of sad ice packs!), or you're brewing a big beer, a starter is an absolute must. If you start brewing some really big beers (8% alcohol or above), you can double the size of your starter (the liquid yeast recipe from above), making 2 litres (70 fl oz) with twice as much malt extract. And if your beer is small, but the yeast is a bit old, you can make half a starter.

As always, try something, take notes and see how you go — with experience, you'll discover what works for you.

# An all-grain brewing adventure

For more ambitious brewers who want to start from scratch, all-grain brewing is the eventual goal. This is brewing from whatever raw materials you want. You aren't limited to extracts that have been prepared for you, with a baked-in fermentability, and there are no bounds on your creativity. This requires additional equipment, time, and a strong grasp of fermentation and sanitisation — and, of course, excellent record keeping.

The growth of the hobby means there are now dozens of equipment options, from DIY mash tuns made from picnic coolers, all the way through to turn-key systems with professional-level controls. There are one-pot, brew-in-a-bag options, and multi-vessel systems that resemble professional breweries. Each has their own nuance, but when armed with the manufacturer's instructions — or advice from one of the many incredibly generous bloggers in the home-brewing world — you will no doubt be able to navigate the process, given the building blocks in this book, and your experience with extract brewing and fermenting.

Chapter Seven

# THE TASTE TEST

Some of your mates will call this stage of the process 'drinking'; I prefer 'evaluating'. Regardless of what you call it, it's still going to be fun.

Here, we present our beer in the best possible conditions and take in what we've made. We isolate the bad, find the good, and devise a plan of attack for the next brew day. The notes you took throughout your brewing will come in handy here as we try to identify both the faults and the positive aspects, and figure out what to change and what to repeat.

## Set the stage

Beer is an exceptionally complex beverage. Not only does its flavour change in the bottle or keg over time, but it also changes in your glass as your hand warms it and the carbon dioxide vents off. Other factors will also affect your ability to identify flavours, so it's important to be aware of what externalities are influencing your perception of your beer's flavour.

At the biggest breweries with the most involved sensory programs, tasters are placed at cubicle-style desks with plain white walls and separators, to minimise external stimuli and allow the brain to focus. You don't have to go over the top and drain all the fun from enjoying your beer, but do be aware of what could be having an impact on it.

### HOW TO PREPARE FOR YOUR TASTING

→ Chill your beer for at least 24 hours to encourage the yeast to settle out. More time will allow the last few stragglers to settle out. Yeast in suspension will add a meaty flavour and chalky texture. There's nothing wrong with consuming some yeast — a bit of gut biodiversity is important! — but too much yeast will lead to an uncomfortable system and an unhappy partner.

→ Choose a glass that gives you access to the aroma of the beer, with enough excess capacity to let you agitate the beer without spilling it. A large-mouthed red wine glass is perfect, as it's designed for sensory analysis of wine. It's large enough to hold a good volume of beer, is shaped for easy swirling and funnels the aroma up towards your nose.
- Clean glassware will give your beer a leg up. Use a glass that has been thoroughly rinsed with hot water, to strip out any residual detergent on the glass — detergent will break down the foam you worked so hard to build and maintain. If you see bubbles sticking

to the side of your glass, it wasn't properly cleaned. The bubbles are a sign of organic matter stuck to the glass; the matter creates a 'nucleation' point, where dissolved carbon dioxide comes out of solution. Not only is it gross because your glass has crud in it, but it also degasses your beer and affects its flavour.

→ Smoker? Wash your hands. Each time you bring your glass to your mouth, the cigarette smell on your fingers will crowd out the more subtle beer aromas. Cigarettes are also a well-known palate wrecker. Try not to smoke for as long as possible before analysing your beer.

→ Gum chewer? Spit it out. Try eating a plain cracker to help get the minty fresh taste out of your mouth.

→ Now warm your beer. I know I said to chill it, but beer that's too cold will numb your tastebuds and you won't be able to appreciate the nuance of the flavours, good or bad. Warm your beer by just leaving it out of the fridge for about 5–10 minutes. That will take the edge off, and when the beer hits the room-temperature glass it will warm up to perfect tasting temperature.

## Pop the top

With your beer now at a good serving temperature, and your glass cleaned, it's time to taste.

→ Pop the top off your beer. Seems simple, right? But observe what you see and hear. Did you get the typical hiss of a commercial beer as built-up gas escaped? Do you have beer gushing out? The first indicates a well-carbonated beer. If nothing vented out, you may have low or no carbonation. The second indicates an over-carbonated beer. And this over-carbonation may indicate an infection in the bottle that caused excessive gas formation, or you've used too much priming sugar — tasting will tell you which you have.

## Pour the first

→ Pour the first 100 ml (3½ fl oz) of your beer into the bottom of your glass and allow the foam to stabilise.

→ Now tilt the glass and gently ease into the wall of the glass; you're aiming to create about two finger-widths of foam. Pour more aggressively if your foam isn't forming. Pouring this way will open up the beer, build the foam and enable you to fully evaluate the beer.

- It's through the creation of foam that aromas, good or bad, will be carried out of the beer.
- Managing a good pour is a bit of an art and depends on the level of carbonation. A higher-carbonated beer needs less effort to build foam, while a lower carbonation may require the entire beer to be poured into the bottom of the glass, and perhaps from an elevation.
- Don't be greedy: leave the last 10–20 ml of beer in the bottle, as it's rich in yeast.
- Particularly as you poured some, stopped, and poured again, your yeast will have been stirred up in the bottle. Learning to pour without rousing the yeast is something every home brewer should aspire to.
- A visible quantity of yeast will impact your presentation and flavour.

→ Once again, note the activity.

- Did the beer foam out of the glass? If it's over-carbonated, you either need to use less priming sugar next time (perhaps you forgot to adjust down the amount of sugar for a smaller batch size?), or if it also tastes a bit sour, you picked up an infection and need to review your sanitation process.
- Did you struggle to create foam, even with an aggressive pour? You most likely have under-carbonated beer. Try adding more priming sugar next time. (Was your batch bigger than planned, because you over-diluted when you pitched your yeast?)

→ If you didn't get much foam, it could also be that the yeast didn't ferment the priming sugar.

- Were your bottled beers stored cold immediately after bottling? Cold impedes yeast activity.
- Did you cold condition* your beer, and forget to add back yeast?
- Did life get in the way and you couldn't bottle your finished beer when planned? Excessive conditioning will lead to yeast dropping out of suspension. As with cold conditioning, additional yeast may have been needed.

→ Did the foam form, but dissipate very quickly?
- This could be because your recipe was lacking the foaming properties contributed by malts such as wheat, oats and crystal malt. Try the extract plus specialty grains method next time (see page 106), and use some (or more) light-coloured crystal or caramel malt and/or wheat malt.
- This could also be a sign of detergent in your fermenter, bottle or glass. Make sure everything you use is fully rinsed with the hottest water you can safely handle, and that your sanitiser is fully drained from your fermenter and bottle before filling. Chemical detergents are designed to break down and carry away the same compound we rely on for foam creation.

## Smell the beer

→ Stick your nose right down into the rim of the glass, and with an open mouth, breathe in through your nose. Ideally you're getting hits of vibrant hop and sweet malt aromas.

→ Swirl the beer in the glass to encourage more gas to escape, and foam to build, and smell it again. If you like what you smell, congratulations!
- You may detect unwanted or offensive aromas. There are entire books dedicated to sensory analysis, as well as great online resources, to help you identify the cause of these aromas, and put together a plan to avoid them on future batches.

* **Cold conditioning, or cold maturation, is the process of maturing beer in a cold environment. It's another term for lagering. When you store beer cold, you encourage yeast to drop out of solution. So in this advanced technique, you will have a beer that doesn't have enough yeast to properly 'bottle condition', and yeast will need to be added back in at the time of packaging.**

→ The following are a few main home-brewing aroma faults to watch out for.

- **Sulfur** — this is a clear sign of yeast stress. It can usually be detected before bottling, and letting the beer mature longer will allow it to vent off. If it's in your finished beer, all is not lost. Swirling the glass will help to vent it off.
- To avoid sulfur in your next batch, make sure the wort is in the correct temperature range when you pitch your yeast.
- Make sure your wort was been aerated to the best of your ability. Pour the wort slowly into the bottom of the fermenter to splash it as best you can for as long as you can. You may also look into mechanical aerators at your local home-brew shop or online.
- Maintain a good fermentation temperature. This can be very hard and may even mean you can't avoid this aroma when brewing in very hot or very cold times of year.
- Use fresh yeast that has been properly stored.
- Use enough yeast. A single packet of yeast is good for a 21 litre (5½ gallon) batch of beer up to around 6%. A bigger batch, or one with more alcohol potential, needs more yeast.

- **Phenols** — these can come from ingredients, chemicals or yeast, and at low levels can be desired or pleasant. At higher levels they can be perceived as a 'band aid' or medicinal.
- Phenols may have come from the water you added to dilute your beer after the boil and cooling process. If you used plain tap water, try boiling it the day before without a lid, or use bottled water. You may have introduced too much chlorine.
- They may also have come from poorly rinsed equipment. Make sure all detergents are rinsed thoroughly with the hottest water you can safely manage. Ensure you're using no-rinse sanitisers, and that fermenters and bottles are allowed to drip-dry for a reasonable amount of time before being filled with beer.

## The three-sip rule

1. Never judge a beer by the first sip. The first sip is setting the stage. It has to contend with the other flavours sitting on your palate already, as well as with your brain and its expectations.
2. The second sip aids in washing the palate of contending flavours.
3. By the third sip, your brain is able to focus solely on what is in the beer you're tasting.

- Wort-spoiling bacteria can also lead to phenols when they are able to colonise your wort before the yeast does. Use enough ice to cool your wort as quickly as possible. Keep the kettle covered during cooling, and don't lift the lid or put anything that hasn't been sanitised in your wort — beat back any friend who tries to dip their fingers in it for a taste!

→ If your beer is lacking hop aroma, here are a few things to consider.
- Old hops — stale hops don't have the aromatic properties of fresh ones. Try using the hops your home-brew shop packaged most recently. They may not be exactly the variety your recipe calls for, but a fresh hop of the wrong variety trumps a stale hop any day.
- Adjust your hop additions: increase the quantity used later in the boil, or post boil, so the aroma isn't being boiled off.
- Try a dry hop.
- Remember to rack and bottle your beer gently. Aggressive racking or bottling will agitate the beer, which degrades foam creation in the finished product, and volatises your precious hop aroma. Rack and bottle slowly and gently.

## Taste the beer

It's been roughly four weeks of anticipation and you've earned it! Beer flavour is the final part of the beer tasting experience after visual and aromatic observation.

Beer flavour is the result of the balance of malt sweetness and hop bitterness, layered upon yeast-derived esters and phenols, as perceived by the palate in the absence of distraction from 'off' flavours.

→ Is the taste malty and sweet, or bitter and hoppy?

→ Overly bitter beer can be compensated for in the next batch two ways.

# *Share the love*

The home-brewing community encourages exploration and knowledge sharing. There's an unwritten rule among home brewers that no question goes unanswered and no technique is kept a secret. We all come into the hobby and learn from those before us — we benefit from their mistakes and leapfrog to tackling the next quality improvement. And when we discover a process that improves our beer, we share it.

Collaborating to create a better standard for beer is at the core of what home brewing is all about. Sure, there are competitions with one beer selected as the best — but even if you were told the secrets to how to make award-winning beer, you'd still have to do it yourself. In brewing, knowing what to do is easy, but having the care and attention to do it are not. So there is no reason to keep information from each other. And that's what it's all about — collaborating and sharing knowledge levels the playing field so everyone has the opportunity to make great beer.

Amazingly, this knowledge sharing has been absorbed into the commercial 'craft' brewing world as well. Competing businesses are working together to improve each other's products. What other industry does that happen in? As home brewers have moved into bigger systems and begun commercial breweries, there has been a sense that a rising tide lifts all ships. By sharing knowledge and making sure all brewers meet a minimum standard, there is less risk that a consumer will try a bad beer from one brewery and write off craft beer altogether. And welcoming more drinkers into the craft brewing world means each brewer's piece of the pie is bigger. Brewers can afford to run their businesses and make innovative products, home brewers get access to new processes and ingredients, and consumers can have good beer experiences.

Everybody wins.

- One is to reduce the quantity of hops, or the contact time of the hops in the boiling wort — so, you can try reducing the quantity of hops added at the beginning of the boil, or try moving the hops added at the beginning of the boil to a later stage in the boil.
- The second is to build the body of the beer, so there is more residual sugar in the finished product to balance the bitterness.
- It's fairly common for extract-based beer to finish quite dry and thin. Using steeping grains in the crystal or caramel family will add to the residual sugar and body of the beer.

→ Overly sweet beer means it didn't ferment fully, insufficient hops were added to balance the residual sugar, or the bottle re-fermentation didn't happen.

→ Yeast health is a contributing factor to an incomplete fermentation. If the beer tastes or smells of sulfur, indicating yeast stress, then it's a pretty good sign the yeast couldn't complete the job, leaving the beer not fully fermented.
- Try pitching more yeast next time, and make sure you've properly hydrated it with water that is at the right temperature.
- Make sure you aerate your wort to the best of your ability before pitching your yeast.
- Temperature impacts yeast — if the temperature was too cold, it's possible your yeast was coaxed into hibernation before the fermentation was completed.
- Try to avoid temperature shocks to the cold side during fermentation.
- If your house is subject to dropping temperatures, try wrapping a blanket around the fermenter to insulate and trap its natural temperature inside. You could also try using a temperature-controlled heat mat or heat belt — but make sure it has a temperature control, otherwise you can make it too warm.

→ Insufficient hop additions will leave a beer out of balance and tasting sweet.

Beer flavour is the result of the balance of malt sweetness and hop bitterness, layered upon yeast-derived esters and phenols.

- If you don't detect any fermentation issues, indicating a complete ferment, try adding more hops at the 60 minute mark, or start of the boil. This will increase the hop bitterness, which will offset and balance some of the sweetness.
- Hops lose their bittering potential over time, so once again, watch out for old hops. Manufacturer-packaged hops will last for a few years when stored cold and sealed in their original packaging. Ask your home-brew shop when they broke down the package into the small bags they sold you, and build a beer around the freshest hops they have.

→ If your beer tastes sweeter now than it did before you added priming sugar on bottling day, and the beer is flat, the sweetness you are tasting is the priming sugar, because the beer didn't re-ferment in the bottle.
- Turn a sealed bottle upside down and up to a light. If there is a ring of yeast being re-suspended into the beer, then you have yeast and it will probably start fermenting if stored at the right temperature.
- If you don't have a layer of yeast, you may not have enough cells in the beer to re-ferment. Leave it at a good fermentation temperature for a few more weeks to allow the few cells in suspension to complete the work.
- If you left the beer to mature for a few extra weeks, the yeast may have dropped out of suspension in too great of a quantity, and was left behind when the beer was racked. Next time you run that risk, either add some yeast at bottling, or try tilting the fermenter towards the tap when racking to the bottling bucket, to take some yeast with you. An amount that looks like a teaspoon of yeast slurry is sufficient — but don't actually use a teaspoon, as that can introduce bacteria and contaminate the beer; just guess.

→ Does the beer taste overly yeasty, or have chunks of yeast floating in it? With the exception of the witbiers and hefeweizens, yeast doesn't belong in beer in any significant quantity. In most other beers, we want to reduce the amount of yeast in the glass. To do this:

- Carefully rack your beer, monitoring the amount of yeast coming through, and leaving as much as you can behind. If yeast is coming through the hose when you open the tap, you have a tap that's placed too low, or you had an active ferment that created a lot of yeast. Divert the first yeasty bit away from your bottling bucket and throw it away. Tilt the fermenter away from the tap, so gravity pulls the yeast towards the back of the fermenter. Then rack the remaining clean beer.
- Pour your finished beer carefully. You are decanting the beer off the yeast. Be aware of the yeast on the bottom and try to pour without ever standing the bottle back up, until you've decanted all the beer you intend to.
- Store your finished beer cold for enough time for the yeast to drop out, and in a place where they won't be regularly disturbed. This will help form a dense ring of yeast at the bottom of the bottle that is less likely to come out when pouring.

→ Does the beer taste like movie theatre popcorn? **Diacetyl** is a very common flavour compound in insufficiently matured beer.

- Diacetyl smells and tastes like butterscotch or movie theatre popcorn butter, and when present in beer at too high a concentration, it can really get in the way of the enjoyment of beer.
- It can easily be avoided by giving your beer enough contact time with yeast after the visibly active stage of the ferment is completed. When your fermented beer is given time in contact with yeast after the fermentation is complete, diacetyl is reabsorbed by the yeast and broken down into other flavour compounds your tastebuds will not be able to detect.
- Give your beer at least 48 hours after the airlock stops bubbling for the yeast to complete its work before racking the beer off the yeast.

→ Does your beer taste like cardboard?

- While we love oxygen before the yeast is added, we want to avoid it at every stage after that. Without the use of pressure vessels and inert gasses to displace the oxygen, we have to rely on gentle racking processes, and our yeast to scavenge up what oxygen does get picked up along the way. Oxygen in fermented beer leads to oxidation, or a staling of beer. Flavours fall flat and dull.

- Make sure your fermenter is properly sealed during fermentation. When the yeast finishes and $CO_2$ production ceases, oxygen will try to creep into a poorly sealed vessel.
- When racking to the bottling bucket or secondary maturation vessel, make sure your hose is touching the bottom of the bucket you're racking into, and hold it to the bottom until the beer level is above the output of the hose. This is to minimise splashing and the subsequent oxygen pickup.
- On the plus side, the yeast that is still in suspension through to the bottle-conditioning phase will attempt to absorb any oxygen that creeps in — after all, mother nature does want us to have good beer!

What you learn from evaluating your beer will help you to improve your process and recipes going forward. Your goal in brewing is to have your beer ready to drink as early as possible — in the case of bottle-conditioned ales, this will take roughly 4 weeks (and 6–7 weeks for bottle-conditioned lagers); with force-carbonated kegged ale, you can achieve this in 14–16 days (or 4–5 weeks for lagers).

If your beer doesn't taste ready to drink in that time, give it more time to mature at a warm temperature, to encourage the yeast to continue to act and evolve the flavours. And do some homework while you wait. There are countless books that devote more pages than we can here to specific aspects of the brewing process and materials — there is always more to learn.

Share your beers with your fellow home brewers, with home-brew shop owners, local brewers and at home-brew club meetings. The brewing community supports each other and shares knowledge with the common goal of better beer. You are now a brewer and a member of that community.

Don't be shy — get amongst it, be open about your process and about learning. Never stop trying to grow as a brewer, and always be open to helping someone else starting their journey after you.

WHAT NEXT?

Chapter Eight

FERMEN

AMERICAN PA
ELSIE
JUST BEER
WEST COAST I
TINY COCONU
XXPA
MARRICKVILLE
HOPPSY MOZ
2 PEACH SHA
XPA
SUMMER FA
CHAPEAU

The recipes you follow early in your home-brewing journey should be for simple styles like a brown ale, amber ale, or pale ale, as simple versions of these require only malt extract and a single hop variety. A recipe that's too specific, like a hop-forward IPA from your favourite commercial producer, is going to be a challenge, and may result in a letdown, as you don't have the controls they do — so my advice is to keep your target more general and focus on your processes of sanitation and fermentation. These early beers are building blocks while you gain experience and knowledge.

Think about what motivates you and what you want from this hobby — but don't think too hard. This book and hobby are meant to be fun. And you're not deciding on a tattoo or a spouse; you can change your mind at any time. We just need to pick which of two strategies you're going to start with (see page 205 onwards), so we can arm you with the tools you'll need to brew beers that will make you happy.

I continue to tweak my recipes and processes as my suppliers evolve their processes and introduce new products, and as I collect more data on how my system works and my materials interact. Brewing is a journey and every batch has a different set of variables. The trick to improving your beer is keeping those variables as tightly controlled as you can, and changing only one at a time to understand how it impacts the flavour.

As a home brewer, you may not have the ability to control all the variables, but you don't have to, provided you have a realistic expectation of progress, can keep records, and learn to distinguish where the aspects of the change in flavour came from — i.e. is it something you can control? Or is it the result of a variable outside of your control?

## Reading beer recipes

Beer recipes are a description of what ingredients go into making a beer (see page 204), and when applicable contain a few key process features that are outside what's considered the standard brewing process.

Brewing beer is a process, and almost every brewer does the details of the process differently, so rather than providing instructions on the part we all do a little different, a beer recipe is a high-level summary of what you're targeting. It's kind of like telling your friend to meet you at a pub at a given address in a given suburb, but not telling them which bus or train to take — you assume that since they can read a map (in this case, make beer) they will get to where you've told them to meet you.

## Beer name

Starting gravity (SG)
Finishing gravity (FG)
Apparent attenuation
Alcohol percentage (ABV)
Volume (final batch size)
Boil length

## Base malt

Grams of malt extract and variety
– light, amber, dark, wheat

## Specialty grains

Grams of crystal malts
Grams of kilned malts
Grams of roasted malts
Grams of sugar

## 60 minute hop addition

Grams of hop A
Grams of hop B

## 15 minute hop addition

Grams of hop A
Grams of hop B

## 0 minute (flame out) hop addition

Grams of hop A
Grams of hop B

## Dry hop addition

Grams of hop A
Grams of hop B

## Yeast and fermentation

Pitching temperature
Yeast variety
Primary ferment and maturation days
Secondary conditioning days
Priming sugar amount (for desired $CO_2$ levels)

An all-grain version of the recipe would be slightly different, as it would:

- substitute malt extract for a variety or varieties of malt
- have a mash temperature. Mash temperatures to achieve a desired fermentability and attenuation vary by system, so it's best to read what the target final gravity is, and use your experience on your system to determine what temperature to target.

## Strategy 1: Explore, learn, and most importantly, relax

In this style of brewing, you're going to go with what moves you, so express your creativity and give yourself the benefit of a fairly wide target for what your final beer will taste like.

You're choosing not to drill down on specific attributes of a particular beer style in favour of shooting from the hip, so ignore the naysayer who calls you out for having an amber ale that's too dark. Embrace the pleasure of capturing tons of data on what different malts and hops do, and the freedom to add whatever fruit or spice you want to make your twist on a commercial style of a beer you enjoy.

To do this, you only need to understand the basic format of the recipe (see opposite), and how to interpret that into the brewing process I've laid out for you. Then head to your local bottle shop and pick a bottle from a variety of styles from trusted producers, that have been packaged in the last month or two, and see what inspires you. Try to avoid huge beers with tons of hops or potent fruits, and hone in on simpler examples of traditional styles. Then let your imagination take you beyond those basic styles to what variation you want to try to make.

## Strategy 2: Brewing a style and nailing it

After about ten years of off and on brewing, as I changed cities, countries and continents, I decided it was time to get serious. All the data and taste memories I'd collected from years of mixed results trialling all kinds of malts and hops, process changes, and controlled and uncontrolled fermentation temperatures, formed a great foundation. From there I decided on a recipe and brewed it over and over until I had it down pat.

To nail a style, you're ignoring the world of variety in malt, hops and yeast, and settling in a combination you repeat over and over to master your process. Your focus should be around finding the right balance of malt, hops and yeast esters. To do this you need to control your process, so every time you brew the same recipe you should yield the same result — but change one variable at a time to keep improving the flavour.

You then improve the flavour of that beer by making small tweaks to the amounts of this malt, or the timing of that hop addition, or the

# The Beer Judge Certification Program

The BJCP is a fantastic offshoot of the American Homebrewers Association, an organisation whose goal is to protect the rights of home brewers and expand the hobby. It's a fabulous group that has been instrumental in paving the way for this beer revolution we're living in, as most of the new brewers and breweries have roots in home brewing.

The BJCP is responsible for defining the parameters for well-recognised styles of beer, so that objective standards can be set for judging beers in competitions. These guidelines are publicly available and have become the standard for the home-brewing community globally. The guidelines are written by people who use the information available to them to make the best summary of a style they can. They are not a judge and jury, and do not decide whether your idea of what a style is fits or doesn't fit, nor do they pass judgment on commercial brewers whose beer is labelled a 'pale ale', but actually meets the BJCP standards of an IPA.

The point is, don't be creatively restricted by what the guidelines say. Sometimes the guidelines are wrong, and sometimes the industry evolves past the guidelines. Brew what you want to drink, and call it what you want. The only time you need to pay strict attention to these guidelines is when you're brewing for a competition.

Personally, I'm not big on competitions, and get my constructive feedback from sharing my beers with trusted, honest collaborators. But competitions can be great opportunities for constructive feedback, if they're your thing.

temperature of the wort when pitching your yeast, but don't make any dramatic changes. And change only one variable at a time. By holding all things constant except one variable, you're able to see how that ingredient or process change impacts the flavour. This may take five or more brews as you make one change at a time, but provided they keep resulting in beer that's closer and closer to your goal, you won't get bored.

The wonderful thing about nailing a style is that it actually opens you up to be able to brew almost any style, because nailing a style is about process. Once you can control your process for a consistent and predicable outcome, you can chop and change almost any ingredient and still have an idea of what you'll get as a result. So in a roundabout way, restricting yourself and repeating the same style over and over until you nail it actually leads you to being more creative, as you now have the skill as a brewer to achieve what you set out to.

To do this, you need to brew by the numbers. Bust out that hydrometer I told you to buy back in chapter 4; I deliberately haven't mentioned it until now, because you probably wouldn't have used it anyway. If you don't have one, go get one — ideally one with a built-in thermometer. A hydrometer will enable you to measure the concentration of sugar in your wort or beer.

## USING A HYDROMETER

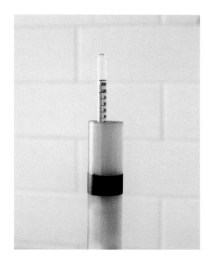

If you're on a boat in the ocean, with no land in sight, on a cloudy day, and you want to know where you're going, you need a compass. Your hydrometer is your compass for brewing. Without it, we're having fun brewing; with it, we know where we're going.

A hydrometer is a long tubular glass device that has numbers running down it, contained within the tube itself. When placed in wort it will float, and the number on the scale that meets the top of the liquid level is the measure of the amount of sugar dissolved in the wort.

Taking a reading using a hydrometer requires a tall thin plastic tube that's longer than the hydrometer itself (they are usually sold packaged in such a tube), filled with a sample of cool wort. The hydrometer is dropped into the wort — carefully, as the displacement may overflow the wort, so do this in a sink — and spun gently to dislodge any air bubbles stuck to it (those air bubbles will hold the hydrometer up, giving you a false reading). The reading is taken and then adjusted based on the temperature of the wort; free temperature adjustment charts are available on the web, such as www.brewersfriend.com/hydrometer-temp/.

**Take readings during each of these steps in the brewing process:**

1. Pre-fermentation — this reading will give you the starting gravity (SG) or original gravity (OG). Make sure you take a sample of wort that is well mixed with the water you used to dilute it.
2. Post-fermentation — this tells you the beer's final gravity (FG), and will confirm the residual sugar and attenuation level. Make sure your sample has been given time to vent off the carbon dioxide, as $CO_2$ bubbles escaping the beer will lift the hydrometer, skewing your result.

When exactly is 'post-fermentation'? You will know this by taking a reading for a few consecutive days when the airlock activity is slowing.  Record your hours from pitching, airlock activity, and reading (adjusted for temperature). Do this for as many consecutive days as required to get a constant result after two consecutive readings. When you see no change in the gravity over that 24 hour period, the yeast is done, the fermentation is complete, and your beer is now in the maturation stage.

## FLAVOUR: MEASURING ATTENUATION AND BALANCING RESIDUAL SUGAR

By measuring the starting sugar levels, or gravity, before fermentation and the finishing sugar levels (gravity), you can calculate the 'attenuation level', and from this you will learn a few things about your beer.

1. What is the quantifiable residual sugar level in your beer? This translates into the amount of sugar you can taste, which plays into your targeted level of hop bitterness and the balance of the two. Residual sugar is also a measurable indicator of the body in your beer, another flavour component perceived by drinkers as weight on the palate; higher residual sugar will feel heavier on the palate, giving the drinker a feeling of being full, while less residual sugar will feel more thin on the pallet and will be less filling in the stomach.
2. How much alcohol is in your beer? As yeast consumes sugar it creates a predictable measure of units of alcohol, so by knowing the starting and finishing gravities, you know the amount of sugar eaten, and therefore the amount of alcohol created.
3. Has the beer fermented to the expected level? Using data from previous brews, and knowledge of the yeast strain's normal attenuation levels, you can tell if the yeast was healthy enough to complete its work, or if you added too much unfermentable sugar through your recipe choice or brewing process.

Brace yourself. Things are about to get geeky. **Attenuation** is the measure of sugar consumed by the yeast, and is therefore a reference to what residual sugar will be left in the beer. It's the most important measure you need to wrap your head around to nail a style.

Residual sugar plays two very important roles when it comes to flavour and drinkability.

1. Residual sugar is the sweetness you taste, and to maximise flavour and drinkability it needs to be balanced by hop bitterness. Balance is incredibly important in beer. Too bitter is not pleasing, and too sweet very taxing. A well-balanced beer is one that leaves you wanting another sip as soon as you swallow the first. Too far in either direction, bitter or sweet, and the taste will linger on your palate, and you'll find yourself putting the glass down and only slowly working your way through it. A balanced beer will be consumed much faster, as the flavour is pleasurable and doesn't linger on the palate, leaving the drinker wanting more.

2. Even when in balance with bitterness, residual sugar can become taxing for the drinker. Sugar is more filling than water and alcohol, so a beer with a higher residual sugar level will be less drinkable because it's more filling. Don't trust me? Just look at the macro brewers' beers. They blend in rice, corn and raw sugar to keep the residual sugar low, resulting in a beer also known as dry.

When you're designing a recipe, and figuring out what balance of bitterness to residual sugar you want to achieve, keep in mind your yeast's expected attenuation level, and what your track record is with that yeast in achieving that attenuation level.

If your beers with that yeast always end up attenuating further (drier, less residual sugar), consider using a little extra crystal malt to contribute more unfermentable sugar to achieve balance.

If you never seem to reach the normal attenuation level from that yeast, you may be using too much unfermentable sugar — so reduce a little crystal on your next batch (or mash a little cooler if you're doing all-grain).

## Pay attention: Apparent attenuation

In the professional brewing world, attenuation is technically known as 'apparent attenuation'. Due to the density of alcohol being lower than that of water, and the presence of alcohol in fermented beer, your measure of sugar remaining in the fermented beer will appear lower than if that amount of sugar was dissolved in water. Casually speaking, it's okay to refer to your attenuation exactly as the numbers indicate (10 units down to 2 means 8 were eaten — 8 is 80% of 10, so your attenuation is 80%), and be aware that what you're really talking about is the 'apparent attenuation'.

## Don't re-create, create: Starting from scratch

Now that you know how to nail a style, branch out and try a few more traditional styles. You'll probably surprise yourself with how easy it is, once you have a consistent process, and you've done a little homework on the new malts, hops or yeast you're using.

Once you have some experience and confidence, put that BJCP style guide and those home-brewing recipe books on the shelf and forget about them. You no longer need to re-create anything — you're ready to go out into the world, put your new skills to the test, and add something to the beer culture in your community.

A new beer idea for me has its roots in an enjoyable drinking experience, and is then influenced and guided by inspiration I draw from culinary experiences, visits to growers of grains, hops, fruit and other sustainably raised food sources, as well as discussions with producers of foods and beverages who share similar values to mine.

I'm driven to discover new combinations of flavours from carefully selected raw materials that can be minimally processed and served as fresh as possible, to give my drinkers the best possible experience. I embrace what's around me to reduce beer miles and celebrate my place.

I hope you come for a visit — first round is my shout. But don't come empty handed. Bring me one of your beers and your story.

With a bit of experience and confidence, you'll be able to craft your own beers. Cheers to that!

# A brewer's glossary

If you're completely new to home brewing, you'll find there's a whole new lingo to learn. Bookmark this page as a quick cheat sheet to refer back to whenever you're feeling a bit bamboozled, and you'll soon be talking beer with the best of them.

**alcohol by volume (ABV)**
The percentage of alcohol contained in a quantity of beer.

**alpha acids**
Compounds within hops that give beer its bitterness. Often expressed as AA%, with lower-value hops lending relatively less bitterness, and higher-value hops being more potent.

**attenuation**
A measure of the sugar consumed by yeast in a fermentation.

**autolysis**
The rupturing of yeast cell walls, and the release of flavour-impacting cell contents. When this occurs at a sufficient threshold, the flavour becomes noticeable. Usually considered as a flaw in beer.

**beta glucan**
A gummy substance naturally existing in cereal grains.

**complex sugars**
Long-chain molecules that are difficult (or impossible) for some yeasts to ferment.

**conditioning**
The process of putting bubbles in beer.

**crown seal**
The cap on a pry-off bottle; a bottle cap.

**diastatic power**
A measure of the enzyme levels in malt. Used as an indication of a malt's inherent ability to convert its contents from starch to sugar in the mash process.

**drop bright**
The action of beer clarification. It can be natural; encouraged with a temperature reduction; and/or assisted with natural or chemical processing aids.

**dry hopping**
The process of adding hops after or during fermentation, to add additional hop flavour and aroma to finished beer.

**flame out**
The end of the boil, when the wort must be treated like a patient with no immune system, due to the risk of bacterial contamination.

**flocculation**
The process of yeast cells bumping into one another, clumping together, and falling to the bottom of a fermenter.

**gravity, or specific gravity**
A measure of the concentration of sugar in a liquid solution. Can be represented as both original gravity (gravity before fermentation), and final gravity (gravity after fermentation).

**hops**
The flower of a plant that lends bitterness, flavour, aroma and antimicrobial attributes to beer.

### India pale ale (IPA)

A very hoppy, sometimes bitter, style of beer with origins linked to the export of beer from England to India, a journey requiring extra hopping (compared to other beer styles at the time), to protect the beer from microbacterial infection. Now a highly popular beer style, focused on accentuating hop aroma and flavour.

### international bittering unit (IBU)

A numerical measure of the bitterness imparted to beer by adding hops. Lower IBU ratings are less bitter, and higher ratings more bitter.

### isomerise (of hops)

The process of binding hop oils to beer, and converting those oils to their characteristic bitter taste.

### krausen

The foam that appears on the top of a ferment, consisting of yeast and protein.

### lautering

The process of collecting wort from grain. Used in 'all grain' brewing and commercial brewing, but bypassed in extract brewing because the malt extract has already undergone lautering when it was manufactured.

### malt

A cereal grain that has undergone the malting process, whereby it is germinated and kilned, to ready the grain for use in a brewery.

### malt extract

A concentrated wort product that enables novice brewers to bypass the first brewing processes, to simplify the brewing process so it can be done in a domestic home kitchen with limited investment.

### mash, mash tun

The process that converts malt's starch into fermentable sugar; also refers to the grain and water mixture in the mash tun (the vessel in which a mash is conducted).

### pitching (of yeast)

The process of adding yeast to unfermented wort.

### racking

The process of transferring beer from one vessel to another, to separate clean beer from the yeast and trub (or added hops or other ingredients) — allowing beer to mature without the risk of those materials contributing negative flavours.

### residual sugar

The sugar remaining in beer after the fermentation is complete. Residual sugar contributes to the sweetness perceived by the drinker.

### saccharification

The process by which enzymes in malt convert the starch in the malt into sugar.

### siphon

A process by which suction creates a flow of liquid from one vessel to another using a hose; can also refer to the tool used to conduct that process.

### sparging

A process of rinsing sugar from the grain after the mash and during the lautering process.

### trub

Coagulated proteins that are created when wort is boiled. Trub can degrade beer quality and flavour when left in contact with beer during a fermentation.

### volatile (compounds)

A term referring to the fragile nature of a compound that can easily be lost through evaporation.

### wort

The sugary liquid to which yeast is added to create beer. The result of the mashing, lautering and sparging processes.

# Index

# Thanks!

Like beer, this book is a collaboration. The pages would be blank without the help of the following collaborators.

Brewers big and small, whose generosity with ideas, processes, successes and failures makes this community and enriches beer culture.

Marrickville, for welcoming us and supporting our dream.

My butcher, for teaching me the importance of soil.

Farmers everywhere, without whom we are nothing.

My sauerkraut maker, for seeing more in me than I saw in myself. This project began in your workshop.

My Batch family, past and present. Your creativity and passion teach and inspire me every day. Your efforts enabled this book. My gratitude is boundless.

Jane, Julie, Katri, Dan, Chris, Rhianne, Lou P., Lou J. and Carol: your guidance, polish, vision, creativity and execution give my words life. I am honoured to have had the chance to work with you all.

My parents, who taught me to work hard and do the dishes — a brewer is nothing if he's not clean.

Andrew, for bringing Batch Brewing Co. to life with me. I'm glad we got to share this journey and I could not have done it without your vision and fortitude.

Bohdan, for whom I work to leave the world fairer and more diverse.

Tory, my collaborator in life. Thank you for your eternal support and for giving me Happiness.